'injuns!'

LOCATIONS

series editors:
STEPHEN BARBER AND BARRY CURTIS

LOCATIONS examines contemporary genres and hybrids in national and international cinema. Each book contains numerous black and white images and a fresh critical exploration of aspects of film's relationship with other media, major themes within film, or different aspects of national film cultures.

on release:

projected cities
STEPHEN BARBER

animals in film
JONATHAN BURT

women, islam and cinema
GÖNÜL DÖNMEZ-COLIN

'injuns!'

native americans in the movies

EDWARD BUSCOMBE

REAKTION BOOKS

Published by
REAKTION BOOKS LTD
www.reaktionbooks.co.uk

First published 2006
Copyright © Edward Buscombe 2006

Printed and bound in Great Britain
by MPG Books Ltd, Bodmin, Cornwall

British Library Cataloguing in Publication Data:

Buscombe, Edward
    'Injuns!': Native Americans in the movies
    1. Indians in motion pictures
    I. Title
    791.4'3652997

    ISBN-10: 1 86189 279 9

contents

introduction

Some time in the late 1980s I was in Taos, New Mexico, at the Indian pueblo. As I wandered around, an Indian man invited me to view his house. Feeling a little embarrassed at intruding into his domestic space, even though invited, I nevertheless inspected the premises, debating all the while if I should offer money. By the time I had finished I had decided that, though his invitation might have simply been an expression of hospitality, it was more likely that it was intended as a transaction and that if he was not too proud to invite me in he was not too proud to accept money. So I offered him some, which he accepted without awkwardness. He then asked if I would like to take his photograph. It so happens that at the time I was trying to write something about photography and Indians, as a way of getting at some ideas around representation of Indians in the movies. I had formed the impression that almost all published photographs taken of Indians had been taken without what we would now recognize as full consent, and that the people taking the photographs had done so with many prejudicial preconceptions: that they had, in short, an agenda. And so I wondered what my agenda would be if I took the man's picture. Unable to convince myself that it would be ideologically pure (whatever that might be), I hesitated and in that moment the chance was lost. Looking back, I regret the opportunity, which I can now see was missed as much through my innate English reserve as much as by political correctness. I would have put the picture into this book if I had taken one.

Attacks on political correctness usually come from those who think they have the right to their prejudices, no matter what. Indians have suffered more from prejudice than most, and if political correctness has helped to change the attitudes of some whites, that is all to the good. But this is not another book pointing out the injustices done to the Indians, nor is it a book describing once more the inaccuracies and distortions that the movies have perpetrated in their representation of Indians. There are already plenty of those. One well-informed writer on the Indians of North America has estimated that by 1997 more than 30,000 books had been written on the subject.[1] Since then the flood shows no sign of abating. So why add to their number? One ought at least to hesitate before pronouncing on a subject seemingly so well worked over.

The same authority also calculates that 90 per cent of these books have been written by non-Indians. I try to imagine how I might feel if 90 per cent of the books on English history, say, were written by foreigners. How much can they really know? They can read the sources, but can they ever really know the English? In recent years it has become commonplace for cultural theorists to question whether an observer from one culture can ever truly understand another. In his ground-breaking book *Orientalism*, Edward Said showed how Western scholars of the Muslim world imposed upon it their preconceptions, finding what they wanted to find, what best fitted in with their prejudices.[2] Study of other cultures is rarely the disinterested investigation it claims to be. Knowledge is power, and the West has always sought to control other worlds through the knowledge it acquired.

If one has the temerity to try to understand another culture, then the difficulties ought at least to be acknowledged. In attempting to get to grips with what is strange, often exotic, are we doing no more than reading into other cultures the assumptions of our own? In trying to make sense of other people who have such a fundamentally different view of the world from our own western, more or less rational and scientific one, we have somehow to translate their world view into a form comprehensible to us. But in so doing are we not inevitably distorting it? As one commentator has put it:

> If the ways of seeing in different communities are in conflict because their interpretive practices reflect incommensurable presuppositions about the human situation, can such communities understand each other? Can one culture use its own terms to say something about another culture without engaging in a hostile act of appropriation or without simply reflecting itself and not engaging the otherness of the Other? . . . can we ever escape our provincial islands and navigate between worlds?'[3]

A further problem is that in order to grasp another culture, we tend to essentialize it, to reduce it to a fixed and unchanging set of principles. This is an ever-present tendency in the representation of Indian cultures, as we shall see. What does it mean to say that Indians have a different mind-set from whites? All of them? Always? Generalizations can be risky. For a start, can one even talk about Indians at all, as a collectivity? As a recent historian has written:

> 'Indian' is not an imported name for a category that pre-dated Columbus; it is a name that brought a new ethnic or racial category into being by precipitating extended, multilateral discourse about the name's meaning. Europeans triggered the discourse when they applied Columbus's misnomer to everyone they found in the Western Hemisphere.[4]

Before Columbus there were no Indians. The indigenous peoples of what is now called North America not only did not call themselves Indians, they did not think of themselves as one people. Only in the process of being collectively identified as Indians by whites have Indians come to think of themselves as having things in common. In this view, Indianness is an artificial construction, imposed by whites. Even the common names of Indian tribes – Navajo, Sioux – are often the names, rarely complimentary, that the whites gave them, sometimes drawing on the derogatory names used by their enemies. Many Indian groups had a name for themselves that translates roughly as 'people' or 'human beings', thus grouping together all other cultures, including other Indian ones, as essentially different, fundamentally other. On the other hand, this present-day Indian identity, though initially imposed by others, is none the less real, since Indians have not been merely passive participants in this process but have played a role in their own self-definition. Contemporary Indians form associations (often using the term Columbus originated, as in the radical group AIM, the American Indian Movement) that are founded on a recognition, or perhaps more precisely a construction, of common identity.

Indian culture these days is fashionable as an antidote to the various ills of western society. Indians are 'ecologically minded', caring for 'Mother Earth' instead of exploiting it. Indian herb medicines offer alternative therapies to chemically produced drugs, while New Age movements and cults draw upon Indian concepts of 'spirituality' to reinforce their doctrines of individual healing and psychic renewal, though their understanding often seems shallow. It's true that certain forms of Indian religion appear to offer a different view of the world from that of the Hellenic-Judaeo one. Whereas Christians ascribe spiritual properties only to human beings, in Indian religion animals, plants and places may all be imbued with spirituality. And whereas Christianity has a chronological basis (Christ lived at a certain point in history), for Indian religions geography is more significant than history. Religion is timeless, but centred on a sacred place, in which can be realized 'the local symbolizations of nature in aesthetic religious forms: in a Sun Dance lodge, in sandpaintings, in pipe bowls, medicine bundles, or ceremonial dress.'[5] However, the attempt to divorce Indian religion from its basis in Indian society, rendering it into a commodity that can be packaged and sold to disaffected middle-class whites, is, as Shari Huhndorf argues, to reduce cultural difference to a mere fad or style.[6] In any case, 70 per cent of Indians profess to be Christians, and so generalizations about Indian religion need to be circumspect.

Much of the current interest in 'Indian' culture is trivial and opportunistic. *Snakedance* (2001), a film directed by Hypatia Lee, announces itself as 'A Fantasy Trip into the Erotic World of the Indian Nation'. It's a porn film that purports to demonstrate Indian sex techniques (though little happens that could not be imagined in the average suburban bedroom). Over shots of birds, trees and grass, titles announce that each of the 'girls' in the film is of Cherokee ancestry. The director appears on screen to pronounce a series of platitudes about Indians' respect for all living things and the value of rituals in cleansing and renewing spirituality, and then refers to 'the medicine wheel, the sacred circular energy which can be honoured in the position more commonly known as 69.' Cut to a couple enthusiastically demonstrating their circular energy.

Yet white western society seems to have an unending curiosity about Indian life, much of it seriously intended. After years in the planning, the National Museum of the American Indian finally opened its doors in 2004. The museum is situated in a brand-new and elegant building situated on the National Mall in Washington, DC, not far from the Capitol. Presenting for view some seven thousand works of Native cultures, the museum announced its mission thus:

> We define a moment of reconciliation and recognition in American history, a time for Indian people to assume, finally, a prominent place of honor on the nation's front lawn. It is our most fervent hope that we will be an instrument of enlightenment, helping our visitors learn more about the extraordinary achievements of the indigenous people of the Western Hemisphere.[7]

Predictably enough, there was immediate controversy when the museum opened. The building itself met with general approval, but the principles upon which the exhibits are organized have been subject to some damaging criticism. The creators of the museum went out of their way to consult with Indian communities on what should be presented. The response they got is summarized in the museum's published account of itself, *Spirit of a Native Place*:

> First, while acknowledging our deep past, Native peoples want to be seen as communities and cultures that are very much alive today. Second, we want the opportunity to speak directly to museum visitors through our exhibitions and public programs, and to describe in our own voices and through our own eyes the meanings

of the objects in the museum's collections and their importance in Native art, culture, and history. And third, we want the museum to act in direct support of contemporary Native communities.[8]

Not, then, a monument to a dead past, but an aid to activism.

A major part of the museum is filled with displays put together by Indian groups themselves in an exercise of self-representation. This produces some striking exhibits, as well as some banalities. But what we might expect in a museum, an organized, authoritative account of the history of Indian societies down the ages, seems to have been largely sacrificed to the desire to assert the vitality of present-day cultures. In its reluctance to tell a coherent story about the development and destruction of Indian cultures, the museum appears to embrace a new form of political correctness that, instead of insisting on the wrongs done to Indians, wishes only to look on the bright side. The guide announces: 'This exhibition encourages viewers to consider history not as a single, definitive, immutable work, but as a collection of subjective tellings by different authors with different points of view.'[9] Undeniably, much Indian history has been written from a highly ideological, white, perspective and the balance needs redressing. But the museum seems in danger of reducing history to a mere aggregate of competing voices, an extreme form of cultural relativism. Does every voice have the same authority? In practice, both the voices of racist whites and of their victims rising up in protest have been largely omitted in favour of a Panglossian determination to take Indians at face value. When we read about Indian ceremonies that 'If performed faithfully and humbly, these ceremonies ensure successful hunts, plentiful harvests, and natural order',[10] one begins to long for a bit of old-fashioned scepticism and intellectual rigour. As one critic has remarked, the museum all too often 'emphasizes a kind of warm, earthy mysticism with comforting homilies behind every façade, reviving an old pastoral romance about the Indian.'[11]

Perhaps it is inevitable that, given the negativity with which Indians have been viewed for most of their history since Columbus, the museum should over-compensate in producing a perspective that seems to fit in so well with New Age notions of healthy living and deep spirituality. So, nothing about inter-tribal warfare, or about Indian societies' oppression of women. But neither is there as much as one might expect about the terrible things that were done to the Indians in the name of progress and manifest destiny. One exhibit announces: 'Swords, diseases and complex political conditions enabled Europeans to exploit the Americas.' But these themes are not developed. Instead, in another glass case, this one full of rifles, there is this assertion:

> Native desire to adopt new goods drove early encounters between Indians and Europeans. Indigenous people gave up some technologies – pottery, stone knives and leather clothing – and adopted brass kettles, metal tools, and, eventually, guns. Europeans increased their

manufacturing capacity to meet the needs of the new American market. As guns became less expensive, they spread everywhere. Native people made guns their own, using the new technology as they used all new technologies: to shape their lives and futures.[12]

Even in America such a gun-positive account of history must raise some eyebrows. Guns are treated as just another commodity, their adoption a sign of progress. The huge imbalance in weaponry between whites and Indians in virtually every conflict between them, with devastating consequences for the Indians, is ignored in favour of a determination to see Indians not as victims but as controllers of their own destiny.

The present book is not about Indian history or ethnography, but about the more limited topic of the representation of Indians in the movies. It's not about what Indians are really like, or what really happened to them, so much as it is about how white people have chosen to represent them in the most popular and hence influential medium of modern society. Perhaps inevitably, even with the best intentions of being true to one's subject (and it has to be recognized that best intentions have not always been to the fore in Hollywood), films made by white people for white audiences will inevitably produce an image of Indians designed to serve a white agenda. We see in Indians what we want to see, what we need to see. But those wants and needs can be quite complex, and can change over time. This is an attempt to tease out a few of these shifts, through looking at some unfamiliar material, or taking a new look at what appears already well known.

Many previous books about the representation of Indians in the cinema content themselves with labouring a simple form of political correctness, berating Hollywood for the mistakes it makes, its lack of ethnographic or historical accuracy, or its failure to tell the unpalatable truth about how whites behaved towards Indians. In *The Only Good Indian . . . The Hollywood Gospel*, authors Ralph E. Friar and Natasha A. Friar repeatedly accuse filmmakers of ignorantly confusing one tribe with another, or ascribing the ceremonies of one Indian group to another.[13] In *The Pretend Indians: Images of Native Americans in the Movies* John A. Price points up the ethnographic bias in the cinema's almost exclusive concentration on the plains tribes: 'Most American Indians did not depend upon large game as their primary source of food but were in fact agriculturalist. Most American Indians lived in permanent houses, not in temporary hide tents. Most American Indians did not wear tailored hide clothing, but woven robes.'[14] This is well said, and I make the same point myself in these pages. But all too often this kind of critique can descend into a pedantic listing of errors of costumes, props or weapons in films, exercises in tedious point-scoring such as is practised by Ward Churchill in comments on the movie *A Man Called Horse* in his book *Fantasies of the Master Race: Literature, Cinema and the Colonization of American Indians*.[15]

Churchill believes that cinema, by concentrating solely upon a narrow period of time in Indian history, the second half of the nineteenth century, is in effect denying the present-day realities of Indian existence. A somewhat similar point is made by Armando José Prats in *Invisible Natives: Myth and Identity in the American Western*. Prats argues that the Western, by virtue of the fact that it is a historical film, typically places Indians in a kind of time capsule, preserving them as they once were, while ignoring that Indians have continued to develop into the present day. He quotes Robert F. Berkhofer Jr:

> In spite of centuries of contact and the changed conditions of Native American lives, Whites picture the 'real' Indian as the one before contact or during the early period of that contact . . . [M]ost Whites still conceive of the 'real' Indian as the aborigine he once was, or as they imagine he once was, rather than as he is now.[16]

I don't disagree with this observation, though I don't necessarily accept what seems to be the implication, that no one should make historical films, only films about Indians as they are now. This seems simplistic and unrealistic, in that it ignores the pressure of genre in popular cinema, and underestimates the difficulties of persuading a mass audience that films about contemporary Indians are good for them, as well as good for Indians. Prats's fundamental point is that Westerns find it impossible to represent Indians directly, instead always seeing them through white eyes. As a general statement, this is undeniable. Search where you will in the Western, you will scarcely find an Indian whose existence is presented direct, unmediated, without some kind of representative in the film of the white audience. *Chief Crazy Horse* (1955) is basically a biography of the great Sioux leader, with a major Hollywood star, Victor Mature, in the lead part. Nevertheless it feels the need to invent a white character, Major Twist, to mediate between Crazy Horse and the audience, to interpret him for us, as it were. What we have, therefore, is a white view of Indians, produced for white consumption.

Other recent books on the topic, such as *Celluloid Indians: Native Americans and Film* by Jacquelyn Kilpatrick and *Hollywood's Indian: The Portrayal of the Native American in Film*, edited by Peter C. Rollins and John E. O'Connor, make much the same point.[17] The purpose of the present book is not to dispute these arguments, or in any way to redeem Hollywood. I accept that what appears on the screen is, as with representations of Indians before the cinema was invented, an image produced for the purposes of white people. But whereas this is the point at which previous books arrive, after a trawl through the hundreds of films turned out by Hollywood through the years I prefer instead to make this my point of departure, assuming to a great extent that readers will already be persuaded that Hollywood films are not accurate historical records.

In the first chapter I attempt a brief review of early, pre-cinematic attempts to represent the Indian in order to show that the cinema inherited an already predetermined set of ideas and images, that the generic forms of the Western were fixed from the outset, despite some interesting early variations. Working within a genre, filmmakers are not as free as they think they are, or as critics think they are, to choose a more 'accurate' or ideologically 'correct' type of representation. Genre locks in certain images to the exclusion of others.

The next chapter attempts to complicate the question by looking at a number of films that have offered a generally sympathetic or 'liberal' view of Indians. I try to show that the liberal intentions of these films, while by no means a sham, need to be understood in terms of political and other discourses originating outside the cinema. Later films, from the 1960s onwards, though professing a more sophisticated cultural viewpoint, do not necessary mark an advance.

The third chapter considers the curious history of white people passing for Indians, both in the cinema and elsewhere, and considers the reasons for this and what light it sheds upon the history of the Western. In the next chapter I review the not inconsiderable body of European Westerns, in which Indians are often accorded a radically different significance from American examples of the genre. I conclude with an account of another way of looking at Indians, one with an interesting history, though undeniably representing a white point of view. Because of the way the Western developed, this view, perhaps regrettably, was not one that the genre could incorporate.

a note on the title

As every schoolboy knows, Christopher Columbus was confused concerning his whereabouts when he first encountered the indigenous peoples of the western hemisphere, but his designation of them as 'Indians' somehow stuck, and it's a term still in common use today. Many of the descendants of these people continue to refer to themselves as Indians, despite attempts by the politically correct to substitute the term 'Native American'; indeed, a US Department of Labor survey in 1995 found that nearly half of American Indians were happy to be so designated, while only 37 per cent preferred the term Native American. (Just to make matters more complicated, in Canada the equivalent term is 'First Peoples'.) Despite the subtitle of this book, however, I don't think there are any 'Native Americans' in the movies, nor for that matter any Indians either. The popular cinema has not sought to present the reality of Indian lives. Instead it has created a fiction for its own purposes, one which is more accurately labelled 'Injuns', a term the movies themselves popularized, and one which, shorn of any derogatory implications it may have accrued, I employ to signal what this book is, and is not, about: the origins and implications of fictional 'Injuns'.

1 the formation of a genre

I first visited the United States in 1977 to teach in the Midwest at the University of Iowa, a state named after an Indian tribe, although I never saw an Indian the whole time I was there. When the semester was over I drove my car from Iowa to Los Angeles. Being already a keen student of the Western movie, I made sure my itinerary passed through Monument Valley, where I genuflected to the memory of John Ford. We stopped for breakfast at a small café at Mexican Hat, a hamlet at the Utah end of the valley. At one side of the café was a group of people eating. Stocky in stature, with wide, brown faces, they wore jeans and straw cowboy hats. I made a remark to my companion, assuming these people were Mexicans. Don't you know who they are, she asked. She told me they were Indians. By that time I had probably seen several hundred Westerns and thought I knew what an Indian looked like. Obviously I didn't.

Where do white people's ideas about Indians come from? Undoubtedly, the most pervasive and potent contemporary source is the cinema. Throughout most of the history of Hollywood, until it began to lose its appeal in the 1960s, the Western was the major genre of American cinema, comprising between a fifth and a quarter of all feature films made in the period 1910–1960. In the last century something like seven thousand Western feature films were produced in all, and a substantial proportion of these deal with Indians.[1] For every white American who has ever seen, still less met, an Indian, there must be a thousand whose only experience of Indians has been on film. And of course for Europeans this will be even more the case.

Western films, it hardly needs stating, afford a highly skewed version of Indian life. In the first place, they do not reflect the diversity of Indian culture. At the time of the first encounters with whites, there were at least 300 distinct Indian languages in America north of Mexico. The cultures that spoke these tongues lived widely differing existences. In the south-east Indians grew corn in irrigated fields. On the great

Edward S. Curtis, *The Wedding Party: Qagyuhl*, 1915.

plains Indians lived by hunting buffalo – on foot, since there were no horses in the Americas until Europeans introduced them. In the deserts of the Great Basin Indians lived by gathering roots and seeds, constructing temporary shelters from branches and grass. In the south-west the Pueblo Indians lived in multi-storey adobe houses and farmed corn, squash and beans. In the north-west Indians lived in huge log houses and fished salmon in the rivers or went to sea in canoes and hunted whales.

In the movies only a fraction of this diversity gets onto the screen. Representation is confined to little more than half a dozen tribes: Sioux, Cheyenne, Blackfoot, Comanche, Apache, Kiowa, with an occasional appearance by Seminoles, Utes or Shoshone. A small number of films set in the eighteenth century feature Indians of the north-east, such as the Iroquois and Hurons. Oddly, perhaps, given the provenance of the films themselves, the numerous tribes of Californian Indians virtually never appear in the cinema.

The historical spread of the films is as restricted as the geographical one. The great majority of Westerns take place within the period between the end of the Civil War in 1865 and the turn of the century. The effect of this concentration upon such a small segment of history is to freeze the Indians in time. This is the way they have always been, we assume. And since so few films portraying Indians are set in the present day, there is a tendency on the part of white audiences to assume that, unlike the rest of society, Indians have not developed since the nineteenth century.

Often in the cinema Indians, faced with the threat of forcible eviction by whites, speak of their ancestral lands, sacred since time immemorial, as if to confirm that Indian life is immutable. In fact, Indian societies have undergone momentous historical changes, both before Columbus and since. Two things, besides the obvious and shattering effect of white invasion, have most altered Indian society. First was the discovery of how to grow corn, which occurred in Mexico around 3500 BC. By AD 1000 corn had spread up the Mississippi and into the Ohio Valley, enabling large populations to form in permanent townships whose economies were based on agriculture. 'Around the time the Normans were invading England and Christendom was embarking on the first Crusades, Mississippian culture peaked near present-day St Louis with the emergence of the largest town in pre-Columbian North America, a paramount chiefdom unlike anything seen before or since.'[2] This town, subsequently named Cahokia by archaeologists, was constructed of more than a hundred massive earth-mounds, the remains of some still visible today. One covered sixteen acres at its base. The town may have contained ten thousand people. Yet, for reasons imperfectly understood, the civilization based there went into a decline in the fourteenth century, well before Europeans arrived. Hollywood has made scores of films dealing with the ancient civilizations of Egypt, Greece, Rome and elsewhere, but has yet to find pre-Columbian Indians a viable subject.

The second dramatic change in Indian societies came about as a result of horses escaping from the Spanish and gradually spreading over the continent. By 1680 Indians in Texas and New Mexico had their own horses. The result was a complete change of lifestyle for many Indian tribes, who, though still beyond the reach of white domination, benefited from this product of white culture. The Cheyenne had been a corn-growing people before acquiring horses in the eighteenth century and switching to hunting buffalo (for which their language evolved 27 different words depending on the animal's sex, age and condition).[3] Another group, the Numu people, as they called themselves, had originally been based in the northern Rocky Mountains, but the acquisition of horses encouraged them to venture out onto the plains. When the Spanish first encountered them in the eighteenth century they gave them the name used by their Ute neighbours and called them Comanche. By the end of that century their skill with horses (their language had seventeen different words for a horse based solely on its colouring) gave them dominance over much of the southern plains, pushing the Apaches into the mountains of New Mexico.[4] Thus the Comanche who appear so often in Westerns set in Texas, such as John Ford's *The Searchers* (1956), are in fact quite recent arrivals, even more so than the Spanish.

Why does this variety of cultural and historical experience not find its way into the cinema? We must start with the fact that movies are made for the mass audience. At the last census in 2000, the total population of the United States was 281.4 million; the total Indian population was 4.1 million, or 1.5 per cent. (This includes both people who defined themselves as solely of Indian extraction, and those of partly Indian origin.) A film industry aimed at a mass market and dedicated to making profits is not likely to cater for such a small minority if their tastes or interests are radically different from the majority. It does not necessarily follow that Hollywood will seek only to reinforce existing ideas and beliefs; money can sometimes be made by challenging received wisdom. But if, as some would certainly argue, whites' perception of Indians and Indians' perception of themselves are so far apart as to be mutually incompatible, then if forced to choose between the two we would expect Hollywood to make films that are more in tune with the ideas of whites than of Indians. A film whose terms of reference were totally within an Indian mind-set might be a difficult thing for the popular white audience to understand, let alone sympathize with. Hollywood has made scores, even hundreds, of films that have tried to recognize injustice towards the Indians, or see their point of view. But ultimately they have been all from a white perspective. If an Indian 'problem' is recognized, it is always from the standpoint of how is this a problem for white people? How could or should white people deal with it?

Almost invariably, if a film includes Indians, they will be shown in some sort of relationship with whites. Whereas whites in Westerns can comfortably exist without Indians being present, if Indians are shown then we see them in contact with white people, usually in a relationship of antagonism. There are a very few exceptions to this rule, which we shall come to later, but it is clear that by and large Indians are found interesting only in so far as they relate to us, the whites, and not in and of themselves. Interestingly, this is not necessarily the case in other media. In novels Indians are often the subjects, without their needing to be seen in relation to whites. But novels are not a mass medium, or not necessarily so. A novel can be viable with a readership of a couple of thousand people. For a movie, even an audience of a couple of million is judged a failure.

However, it is not simply a matter of what audiences will or won't accept. Film genres, like other cultural products, have a history. There are reasons why genres take the form they do, which have to do with their origins and the circumstances in which they are formed. Genre may be seen as a means of organizing artistic production so as to minimize unpredictability. Audiences need to know, in advance of buying a ticket for a performance, that the film they are going to see is one that will appeal to them. Contrary to what is sometimes asserted, genre films are not 'all the same'. If that were so, they would not supply the novelty that is an essential part of the filmgoing experience. But too much novelty makes it hard to guarantee satisfaction. There must be a level of similarity to those experiences we have pleasurably consumed in the past. If we like Westerns, the chances are that we will like the new one on offer. While this is undoubtedly the reason why genre has such a powerful hold in popular cinema, however, assuring satisfaction to the audience and continuing profits to the producers, and making it possible for the wheels of the industry to keep turning, at the same time genres can take on a momentum that is in part independent of both audiences and producers. Genres have a life of their own, as a result of the specific circumstances in which they come into being.

Thus the reason why Westerns represent Indians in the ways they do is not simply a function of their role as mass entertainment for a contemporary white audience. The genre of the Western began at a particular historical moment, in response to a particular set of circumstances, and this determined to a great extent its special characteristics. The view of Indians that was laid down at the time the genre was formed is still embedded deep within its structure, as the rocks laid down in earlier eras determine the structure of the land above, despite the shaping influences of more recent events such as erosion.

As we shall see, during its development the Western acquired a set of conventions both in relation to its visual iconography and also in terms of its typical narrative structures. Though whites had made pictures of Indians from the sixteenth century onwards, and though there had been stories about encounters with Indians from an equally early date, it was not until the later nineteenth century that the wide range of material, both visual and narrative, that had been gathered up around the broad topic of the American West became codified into the Western genre as we know it, a ready-made set of stories and conventions for the cinema to exploit.

Feature films are first and foremost stories, and in the nineteenth century one of the most popular media for telling stories about Indians was the theatre. James Nelson Barker's play *The Indian Princess; or, La Belle Sauvage*, described as an 'operatic mélo-drame', was first performed in 1808. It relates the story, already familiar at the time, of Pocahontas, the daughter of Powhatan, an Indian chief in colonial Virginia in the early seventeenth century. According to the legend, though modern scholars have doubted its veracity, Pocahontas rescued Captain John Smith from being killed by her people. What is not in dispute is that she subsequently married John Rolfe, journeyed with him to London in 1616, was presented to King James I at court but died a year later, and was buried in Gravesend.

In the play Pocahontas is represented as a true friend of the whites, despite opposition from her compatriots, pleading with her father for Smith's life.[5] Already we have, so common in such stories, the division into good and bad Indians. The good ones are those who help the whites. The beautiful Indian princess (almost invariably an Indian woman needs to be of high birth if she is to be a suitable match for a white man) is already a fixture.[6] Sexual relations between white women and Indian men, if treated at all, are usually regarded as offensive.

Dozens of Indian plays were performed in the 1830s and '40s. George Washington Custis, a foster step-grandson of the first President, produced his own version of the Pocahontas tale in 1830, which continued to circulate the 'myth of the supportive and assimilating Indian'.[7] The year before, one of the most popular of all Indian plays had been premiered. This was John Augustus Stone's *Metamora; or, The Last of the Wampanoags*, which starred the actor Edwin Forrest in a role

Victor Nehlig, *Pocahontas and John Smith*, 1870, oil on canvas.

he was to sustain for many years; the play stayed in the repertory for most of the century. The central character, Metamora, is based upon the historical figure of King Philip or Metacomet, chief of the Wampanoag tribe in New England, who was defeated and killed in a war with the English settlers in 1675–6. In the play Metamora, far from being supportive of the whites like Pocahontas, is a heroic figure of Indian resistance who refuses to give up his land to the settlers. However, Metamora's defiance is made more acceptable to a white audience by virtue of his melancholy premonition of the fate of his people, an early statement of the concept of the Vanishing American, which as we shall see was to become a dominant perspective of the whites on the 'Indian question'. Counselled to hold back from making war against English settlers, Metamora responds with an eloquent but gloomy prediction:

> Yes, when our fires are no longer red, on the high places of our fathers; when the bones of our kindred make fruitful the fields of the stranger, which he has planted amidst the ashes of our wigwams; when we are hunted back like the wounded elk far toward the going down of the sun, our hatchets broken, our bows unstrung and war whoop hushed; then will the stranger spare, for we will be too small for his eye to see.[8]

Finally, having stabbed his wife to save her from the encircling whites, Metamora unleashes the full power of Victorian stage rhetoric before perishing in a hail of gunfire: 'The last of the

Wampanoags' curse be on you! . . . And may the wolf and the panther howl o'er your fleshless bones, fit banquet for the destroyers!'[9]

These two types of Indian, the one who welcomes the whites, who is willing to cooperate and eventually to assimilate, and the one who resists, despite on occasion knowing the hopelessness of the cause, are the twin poles within which most representations of the Indian would fall during the nineteenth century. The latter type, the Indian as savage, untameable, destructive, a threat to whites, had long been a staple figure. He appears in such paintings as John Vanderlyn's *Murder of Jane McCrea* (1802; Hartford, CT, Wadsworth Atheneum), in which a white woman, her right breast exposed, is being tomahawked by two muscular Indians. But though such lurid visions had an increasing currency as the nineteenth century wore on, this was never the only kind of Indian to find a place in the imagination of whites. Indeed, it is questionable whether it was the dominant one early in the century.

Just at the time that Indian plays achieved their maximum popularity on the American stage, the first artists ventured west of the Mississippi. Paintings of Indians had been plentiful enough before that, both portraits of various native dignitaries visiting Washington and reconstructions of historical events, sometimes hostile, sometimes friendly towards Indians. The mood of the first painters to portray the western tribes as they appeared in their homelands, still hardly touched by white intrusion, was very far from being negative. George Catlin, who first ventured up the Missouri in 1832, is a

John Vanderlyn, *The Murder of Jane McCrea*, 1802, oil on canvas.

George Catlin,
*A Crow Chief
on Horseback*,
1844, drawing.

significant figure, painting from real life tribes that had been scarcely known up to that point. He was also a tireless promoter of his work, publishing books and organizing his pictures into touring exhibitions. Catlin was also the first artist to bring to the public images of mounted warriors with feathered headdresses chasing buffalo, and occasionally each other, across the prairie. Although there is no threat to the whites implied in his pictures, he presents Indians as strong, mobile and active, with a culture that is radically different from that of the whites, yet completely viable and self-sufficient.

Catlin's purpose, though in part to make a living from his work, was also to bring to the public's attention the imminent threat to these Indians' way of life, and to preserve at least some record of them before that life was destroyed. In 1841 he published a two-volume work, *Letters and Notes on the Manners, Customs and Conditions of the North American Indians*. In it he explained the purpose of his work:

> I have, for many years past, contemplated the noble races of red men who are now spread over these trackless forests and boundless prairies, melting away at the approach of civilization. Their rights invaded, their morals corrupted, their lands wrested from them, their customs changed, and therefore lost to the world; and they at last sunk into the earth, and the ploughshare turning the sod over their graves, and I have flown to their rescue – not of their lives or of their race (for they are '*doomed*' and must perish), but to the rescue of their

George Catlin, 'The Bear Dance', a lithograph from his *North American Indian Portfolio*, 1844.

looks and their modes, at which the acquisitive world may hurl their poison and every besom of destruction, and trample them down and crush them to death; yet, phoenix-like, they may rise from the 'stain on a painter's palette,' and live again upon canvas, and stand forth for centuries to come, the living monuments of a noble race.[10]

This is an eloquent statement both of the wrongs done to the Indians and of the inevitable decline and disappearance that most whites assumed to be their lot. Catlin's pessimism proved not far wide of the mark, since one of the tribes he painted, the Mandans, was almost wiped out by a smallpox epidemic soon after. Catlin's pictures, charming in their naivety, show Indians engaged in everyday pursuits such as buffalo hunting, dancing or playing ball games, gathering wild rice or racing their canoes. Many of his paintings are portraits, dignified Indians posing in their finery. Generally they appear confident and happy.

So too are the Indians painted by Alfred Jacob Miller, an artist who accompanied a wealthy Scotsman, William Drummond Stewart, on a hunting expedition into Wyoming in 1837, where he painted both Indians and fur trappers. Some of Miller's pictures show Indians fighting each other, but the notion that conflict with whites was the defining characteristic of Indian life is not part of his conception of his subjects. There's a romantic, even wistful look to Miller's pictures, an insight into a secret arcadia, one that would all too soon be intruded upon.

A third artistic traveller of this period was Karl Bodmer, a Swiss painter who joined Prince Maximilian of Wied Neuweid on a scientific expedition into the Dakotas and Montana (as they later became). Bodmer's paintings of Indians emphasize the exotic and picturesque, with Indians performing dances dressed in buffalo masks. It's a tourist's view, though one executed with vigour and élan. A more considered attempt to represent Indian life was made by Seth Eastman, an army officer who, while stationed in Minnesota in the 1840s, made many studies of everyday life among the Indians he observed. Eastman was later commissioned to provide illustrations for Henry R. Schoolcraft's magisterial work *Historical and Statistical Information Respecting the History,*

Seth Eastman, *Lacrosse-playing among the Sioux Indians,* 1851, oil on canvas.

Condition and Prospects of the Indian Tribes of the United States, which was commissioned by Congress and which appeared in six volumes between 1851 and 1857. Eastman's images of Indians playing lacrosse or spearing fish on a frozen lake have both aesthetic appeal and ethnographic interest.

But already in the 1850s the mood was changing. Karl Wimar's painting from this period *Massacre at Wyoming Valley* shows settlers, including a child and an old man, attacked by ferocious Indians armed to the teeth. By now the nature of the white presence west of the Mississippi had altered. Whereas the mountain men who intruded in the first third of the century had no intention of settling in the country, bringing no women with them, but instead frequently forming relationships with Indian women, now, following the discovery of gold in California at the mid-point of the century, emigrants were coming west accompanied by their families, with every intention of settling. Indian hostility was inevitable.

In the period after the Civil War stories of conflict between whites and Indians came to dominate the popular imagination. One sub-genre that achieved widespread currency was the captivity narrative, stories of white men and women who were abducted by Indians. Though the published accounts were often highly coloured, the stories relied for their appeal on their claims to truth, and there was no shortage of instances upon which to draw. The first such narrative to appear was Mary Rowlandson's account of being captured and then rescued during King Philip's War, which was published in 1682. In her anthology *Women's Indian Captivity Narratives*,

Carl Wimar (1828–62), *Massacre at Wyoming Valley*, oil on canvas.

Kathryn Zabelle Derounian-Stodola claims that during the mid-nineteenth century hundreds of women and children were captured by Plains Indians and that there are 'thousands' of Indian captivity narratives in existence, although many are still unpublished.[11] In her book *Captives*, a cross-cultural study of British captives in North Africa, North America and India, Linda Colley records that more than 1,600 New Englanders were seized by Indians and taken to French-held territory between the mid-seventeenth century and 1763.[12] Large numbers never returned home, and some of these chose to remain with their captors, a disconcerting fact for the white societies they had left. Capture in itself might be traumatic, but there is evidence that in time many became acculturated in their new homes.

Mary Rowlandson's story contains no suggestion that she was sexually molested, but by the nineteenth century the popularity of the genre was undoubtedly due in part to the fact that some accounts dwelt on the Indian sexual threat to captured white women. Derounian-Stodola concludes that rape was not in fact widespread; though it did occur, many of the allegations were no more than 'a prurient white fantasy'. Nevertheless, the threat of sexual violation was one that the popular press was only too ready to exploit and the cinema has followed suit. Captivity narratives form the basis of several significant Westerns, such as *Northwest Passage* (1940), *The Searchers* (1956), *Two Rode Together* (1961), *The Stalking Moon* (1968), *Little Big Man* (1970), *Soldier Blue* (1970) and, more recently, *The Missing* (2004), and in each one sexual violation is an ever-present danger.

The first significant writer to use this theme in fiction was James Fenimore Cooper, whose sequence of novels recounting the adventures of his frontier hero Natty Bumppo, variously known as Hawkeye, the Deerslayer or the Pathfinder, was initiated with the publication of *The Pioneers* in 1823. Hawkeye is a man who knows Indians intimately and numbers some of them among his friends, although he is careful to show discrimination. Cooper makes full use of the concept of the absolute distinction between good and bad Indians. The former show signs of civilization and are well disposed towards whites, even helping them against their own

A captivity narrative from 1838.

HISTORY

OF THE

CAPTIVITY AND PROVIDENTIAL RELEASE THEREFROM OF

MRS. CAROLINE HARRIS,

Wife of the late Mr. *Richard Harris*, of Franklin County, State of New-York; who, with Mrs. *Clarissa Plummer*, wife of Mr. *James Plummer*, were, in the Spring of 1835, (with their unfortunate husbands,) taken prisoners by the Camanche tribe of Indians, while emigrating from said Franklin County (N. Y.) to Texas; and after having been made to witness the tragical deaths of their husbands, and held nearly two years in bondage, were providentially redeemed therefrom by two of their countrymen attached to a company of Santa Fe Fur Traders.

It was the misfortune of Mrs. *Harris*, and her unfortunate female companion (soon after the deaths of their husbands,) to be separated by, and compelled to become the companions of, and to cohabit with, two disgusting Indian Chiefs, and from whom they received the most cruel and beastly treatment.

NEW-YORK:

PERRY AND COOKE, PUBLISHERS.

1838.

kind. Bad Indians are those who are savage and hostile and will not recognize the inevitability of white conquest.

Some accounts of the Western genre refer to Cooper as its 'founding father', and there is no doubt that Cooper's novels, in particular *The Last of the Mohicans* (1826), played a major role in popularizing stories set on the frontier, even though for

Cooper the frontier was located in the wilds of upper New York State, back in the eighteenth century. Cooper reinforced the grip that the captivity narrative held upon the popular imagination. The main narrative thread of his best-known book relates the story of Cora and Alice, daughters of a British officer during the wars with the French in the mid-eighteenth century. Twice in the book the girls are captured by Indians, and each time Hawk-eye must rescue them from death and worse. The treacherous Magua, having captured both Cora and Alice, offers to send Alice back to her father on one condition:

> 'When Magua left his people, his wife was given to another chief; he has now made friends with the Hurons and will go back to the graves of his tribe on the shores of the great lake. Let the daughter of the English chief follow, and live in his wigwam forever.'
>
> 'However revolting a proposal of such a character might prove to Cora, she retained, notwithstanding her powerful disgust, sufficient self-command to reply, without betraying the weakness.
>
> 'And what pleasure would Magua find in sharing his cabin with a wife he did not love; one who would be of a nation and color different from his own? . . .'
>
> The Indian made no reply for near a minute, but bent his fierce looks on the countenance of Cora in such wavering glances that her eyes sank with shame, under an impression that, for the first time, they had encountered an expression that no chaste female might endure.[13]

Cora makes it clear that she would prefer to die rather than accede to Magua's demand, thus literally regarding sexual congress with the Indian as a fate worse than death, a view with which her sister concurs when Cora tells her what Magua has offered. At the end, Cora is once more Magua's prisoner, and once more he offers her a choice between 'the wigwam or the knife'. But before she can choose, Cora is spared the worse fate, stabbed to death by one of Magua's companions.

Cooper was writing for an educated, middle-class audience. Two things were needed before the Western could achieve its status as the major national genre. First was the rise of what later came to be called mass communications. Second was the increased interest in frontier conflict as a subject for popular entertainment, consequent upon the renewed pressure upon the western Indian tribes in the period after the Civil War, as a result of the increase in emigration.

In the second half of the nineteenth century advances in printing technology led to the growth of mass-circulation magazines such as *Frank Leslie's Illustrated Newspaper*, founded in 1855, which achieved a circulation of 100,000, and *Harper's Weekly*, founded in 1857 and with a circulation of 200,000 by 1860. Cheap paper produced from wood pulp became readily available from the mid-1850s and steam-driven rotary presses, introduced in the 1860s, transformed the economics of magazine production, enabling the rapid and cheap printing of large numbers of copies. The invention of the Linotype and Monotype machines in the 1880s mechanized typesetting, thus further increasing production speeds and reducing costs. At this time the illustrations used in the magazines, whether drawings or photographs, had to be rendered into engravings before they could be printed, which meant that artists continued to be in demand as a source of pictures. Eventually, in the 1890s, technology evolved to allow the printing of photographs as half-tones, though photography was still a cumbersome process, ill-adapted, through its slow film speeds and heavy equipment, to recording rapid movement.

Developments in production technology would have had a limited effect had it not been for the simultaneous and explosive growth of the railroad system in the period after the Civil War. The first transcontinental railroad was completed in 1869, and soon a network of railroads served the nation, east and west, thus facilitating the rapid distribution of printed material across the country. For the first time the United States formed a unified, modern market, thus making possible a truly national publishing industry.

The new magazines packaged a mixture of reportage, travel accounts, fiction and general interest features on a variety of topics. One of the most popular subjects was the struggle against the western tribes by the US Army. Just when the mass circulation of magazines, newspapers and books had become technically and economically feasible, the level of activity on the frontier was increasing. Conflict between Indians and whites had been intermittent for centuries, and by the early nineteenth century the Indians of the eastern United States were mostly pacified, displaced or destroyed. After the distractions of the Civil War, attention turned in the mid-1860s to clearing for settlement the Great Plains area, between the Mississippi and the Rockies. United States government policy had once considered this the natural home of the Indians, but now the intention was to confine the nomadic tribes to reservations and destroy their power. There were a dozen major campaigns between 1865 and 1891, including the Modoc War of 1872–3 in Idaho and northern California, the Red River War of 1874–5 against the Comanche and other tribes of the southern plains, the campaign against the northern Cheyenne and Sioux in Wyoming and Montana, which included the Battle of the Little Big Horn in 1876, the Nez Percé War of 1877 in Idaho and Montana, and the campaign against Geronimo and the Apache in Arizona and New Mexico in 1885–6. In all, the army recognized 930 recorded fights between soldiers and Indians in this period. For the most part the numbers involved were small, relative, for example, to the immense slaughter of the Civil War. In all the army suffered 932 killed and 1,061 wounded between 1866 and 1891. Total Indian casualties are not recorded.[14] But these struggles caught the imagination of a public eager for thrilling action, and also for stories that seemed to confirm the doctrine of Manifest Destiny, the inevitable and irresistible spread of white civilization across the continent.

At the same time as magazines began to flourish, the dime novel enormously increased the popular market for fiction. Not all dime novels were about the West, but a substantial proportion were set in a fantasy land west of the Mississippi peopled by savage Indians, outlaws, heroic scouts, cowboys and adventurers of all kinds, with a constant supply of maidens in distress for them to rescue. The first of the dime novels, so called because they retailed at the low price of ten cents, appeared in 1860. Its title was *Malaeska, the Indian Wife of the White Hunter*, published by Beadle & Co. and written by Mrs Ann S. Stephens, already a professional and prolific writer. Significantly, as its title suggests, it told a tale of a white man and Indian woman, caught up in racial conflict.

The same year another dime novel appeared. *Seth Jones; or, the Captives of the Frontier* was written by Edward S. Ellis, an unknown nineteen-year-old author. Its huge success, selling over half a million copies, helped to establish the dime novel as a profitable enterprise. Seth Jones is a rough-hewn frontiersman and Indian fighter who eventually proves to be a gentleman, Eugene Morton, just in time to marry Mary Haverland, the sister of a woodland pioneer, Alfred Haverland. In his disguise as Seth, the hero advises Haverland of his views on Indians: 'I tell you, it won't do to trust an Injin. They're obstropertous [*sic*]. Go to put your finger on them, and they ain't thar.'[15] Predictably, the Indians prove treacherous and ferocious. Seth is captured and tormented by one of them, and has no hesitation in wreaking vengeance:

> The savage who had inflicted all this agony seated himself directly behind the chief. Seth stepped to him, and grasping his arm pressed moderately. The Indian gave a scornful grunt. Seth then stooped and gently took the tomahawk from his belt. He raised it slowly on high, bent down till his form was like the crouching panther

The cover of a reissue: *Seth Jones; or, The Captives of the Frontier*, August 1885.

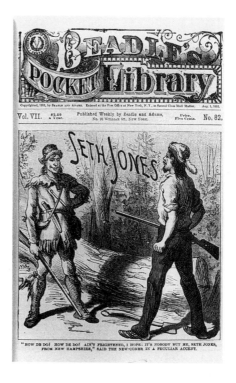

ready to spring. The glittering blade was seen to flash as it circled through the air, and the next instant it crashed clean through the head of the unsuspecting savage![16]

In the course of the next few decades literally thousands of dime novels were published, hundreds of them relating sensational stories of violent struggles against the Indians. In

1877 came *Deadwood Dick, The Prince of the Road,* the first adventure of what was to prove, with the exception of Buffalo Bill, the longest-running fictional hero in dime-novel format. Its author, Edward L. Wheeler, wrote 33 Deadwood Dick books before 1884; after his death further books in the series appeared.

Deadwood Dick: The Prince of the Road appeared in the immediate wake of the defeat of General Custer by Sioux Indians under Chief Sitting Bull at the Battle of the Little Big Horn in 1876. In *Seth Jones* Haverland's young daughter, Ina, is captured by Indians, though there is no reference to imminent rape. But in *Deadwood Dick* the threat is overt and pruriently expressed. Out on the plains, 'midway between Cheyenne and the Black Hills', Fearless Frank, one of the novel's heroes, hears cries for help. He goes to the rescue:

> Securely bound with her face towards a stake, was a young girl – a maiden of perhaps seventeen summers, whom, at a single glance, one might surmise was remarkably pretty.
>
> She was stripped to the waist, and upon her snow-white back were numerous welts from which trickled diminutive rivulets of crimson. Her head was dropped against the stake to which she was bound, and she was evidently insensible.
>
> With a cry of astonishment and indignation, Fearless Frank leaped forward to sever her bonds, when like so many grim phantoms there filed out of the chaparral, and circled around him, a score of hideously

painted savages. One glance at the portly leader satisfied Frank as to his identity. It was the fiend incarnate – Sitting Bull![17]

Fearless Frank rescues the maiden, his first act being to restore her modesty: 'Gently he laid her on the grass, and arranged about her half-nude form the garments Sitting Bull's warriors had torn off, and soon he had the satisfaction of seeing her once more clothed properly.'[18]

The crudeness of the writing and the stereotyped nature of the situations and characters cannot detract from the fact that the sheer volume of dime novels, the thousands of titles produced and the millions of copies circulated, must have had a powerful effect in fixing certain ideas of Indians in the popular mind. And though there are exceptions, the overall impression of Indians that the novels convey is that they are, in Fearless Frank's words, 'savages', 'barbarians', 'cruel captors'.

One of the crucial elements in the formation of a genre is surely the sheer amount of material produced, repeating over and over again the same basic images and situations until they become second nature to writers and readers. For this the dime novel was ideally adapted. As Bill Brown has observed, the mass production techniques used in the physical production of these volumes found an analogy in the systematic regulation imposed on the creative processes involved:

[O]nce the system of the fiction factory was firmly in place, the novels tended to betray their mode of production in the very structure and rhythm of plot construction deployed less to achieve narrative resolution than to sustain tension and generate as many dramatic scenes of confrontation as possible. In other words, plot became a means of producing successive theatrical tableaux. Instead of an integrated and progressive unfolding of events, distinct plots alternated until the denouement; the novel depended on a pattern of event and disclosure, with action in one chapter requiring a subsequent chapter's explanation, and with fragmentation and digression succeeded by hasty, retrospective reconstruction. The technology that produced the Western was completed by the narrative technology of the Western itself – a set of interchangeable parts, a standardized structure, and a regularized rhythm of crisis and resolution, event and explanation.[19]

This description of dime novel production would fit equally well for the production of series Westerns, which remained a staple of Hollywood until well into the 1950s. In the series Western, and even more so in the serials, which feature instalments of a continuous narrative on a weekly basis, plots and narrative incidents were recycled, the hero played by the same actor each time and therefore unchanging, and the other roles selected from a limited repertoire of types, prominent among which was that of the savage Indian.

Dime novels were lightly illustrated, with a few woodcuts. But visual representation of dramatic narratives of the frontier became an important selling-point in the illustrated magazines that emerged contemporaneously. One of *Harper's* foremost illustrators was Frederic Remington, who followed several campaigns against Indians in the west in the later 1880s, sending back both illustrations and written accounts of military engagements. As a professional magazine illustrator Remington was bound to produce what images the market required, and there was no doubt that accounts of dramatic and stirring action were what sold. Remington in any case had little interest in Indian culture as such. In all his many hundreds of pictures, there is scarcely a single one that includes a woman or child or any kind of domestic activity. But as a painter of horsemen, and especially horsemen in battle, he had no rival. Through Remington's pictures the Indian Wars caught the imagination of the public and became a paradigm for the representation of Indians generally. The way Remington showed Indians – half-naked mounted warriors with feathered war bonnets, brandishing lances or tomahawks – was the way the public came to see them, and the mass circulation magazines that commissioned pictures by Remington and his imitators ensured that these images achieved widespread currency. It's not that other images of Indians were not available, as we shall see; but images of plains Indians in warlike action were the ones that chiefly excited the public's imagination, and which, to a great extent, drove out all others.

Remington's is largely a narrative art, which in certain ways anticipates the cinema. Although he did portraits, he showed no interest in the possibilities of Western landscape.

Instead, Remington's most striking pictures show events, either the prelude to an act, emphasizing narrative tension, or a snapshot of action frozen in time. In his picture *The Scout: Friends or Enemies?* (1902–5) a solitary Indian sits on his horse, staring at a barely perceptible line of figures near the horizon. The diagonal line across the centre of the picture formed by the Indian and his horse emphasize the strong tension that the image communicates. Two courses of action will ensue, depending on the answer to the question posed by the title. Implicit in the picture is the idea that out west conflict is the norm. *Downing the Nigh Leader* (1907; Denver, co, Museum of Western Art) is an image familiar to all lovers of the Western, an archetypal confrontation

Frederic Remington, *The Scout: 'Friends or Enemies?'*, c. 1890, oil on canvas.

Frederic Remington, *Downing the Nigh Leader*, c. 1890, oil on canvas.

between Indians and whites in which an Indian is about to bring down the leading horse of the team pulling the stagecoach, with consequences for the occupants that need no spelling out, having been absorbed through countless repetitions down the years in film and other media. In *Captured* (1899) a white man sits half-naked by a fire surrounded by Indians. His arms are bound tightly behind his back. The picture summons up our worst fears as to his subsequent fate; if there should be any doubt, one Indian stands holding a knife, his face implacable.

Henry Farny, another popular artist who like Remington published in *Harper's Weekly*, produced a similar painting in 1885. Entitled *The Captive*, it shows a white man, again stripped to the waist, spread-eagled on the ground, his hands tied to wooden stakes. Sitting at his feet, wrapped in a blanket and with a rifle in his lap, is an Indian, who watches intently. Since in each case the captives are male, the threat of rape is not manifest (homosexual rape being well outside the bounds of publicly acceptable discourse at the time). However, a painting by Eanger Couse, one of the Taos School artists whose pictures generally conveyed a more positive, albeit still white-centred, view of Indians, presents an image exactly in keeping with the lurid fantasies of the dime novelists. *The Captive* (1892) shows a white woman stretched out on the ground inside a tepee. She wears a white dress, the sleeve slightly blood-stained from a wound on her wrist; her hands are tightly bound to a cord about her waist. Her feet too are bound. An Indian, in a blanket and wearing a solitary feather, sits cross-legged by her side, staring at her intently. There are weapons by his side. One of the woman's knees is slightly bent and turned outwards, as if suggesting her

Henry Farny, *The Captive*, 1885, gouache.

Eanger Irving Couse, *The Captive*, 1892, oil on canvas.

defencelessness against the sexual threat; the blood on her body and clothes is emblematic of the implied violence.[20]

Employing many similar motifs, the Wild West show achieved vast popularity in the period between the mid-1880s and the beginning of the First World War. In 1869 a writer going under the pseudonym of Ned Buntline (real name Edward Z. C. Judson) met an army scout called William Frederick Cody. Judson subsequently wrote a story about Cody called *Buffalo Bill: The King of Border Men*; within a couple of years Cody was appearing on stage back east, reliving his exploits out west, which increasingly owed more to the imagination of his writers than to his own real-life experiences hunting buffalo and scouting for the army. Beginning in 1876 Prentiss Ingraham and others wrote literally hundreds

Buffalo Bill and the cast of his 'Wild West' in the arena, 1906.

of dime novels about Cody, turning him into a national institution and laying the foundations for his Wild West show, which contributed hugely to the popularization of the West as a theme for mass entertainment and which was launched in 1883.

Cody's show, in its fully developed form, was a mishmash of separate elements strung together in a fairly arbitrary fashion and mostly derived from rodeo, the circus and from the stage, some of them with at least a tenuous relationship to real historical events. The programme for the 1893 season lists the sharpshooting acts of Annie Oakley, Johnny Baker and Buffalo Bill himself, horse races, demonstrations of trick riding and of bronco-busting, an enactment, complete with live animals, of a buffalo hunt, and a number of crypto-narratives involving Indians. Thus item five is billed as 'Illustrating a Prairie Emigrant Train Crossing the Plains. Attack by marauding Indians repulsed by "Buffalo Bill" with Scouts and Cowboys.' Item thirteen is 'Capture of the Deadwood Mail Coach by the Indians, which will be rescued by "Buffalo Bill" and his attendant Cowboys.' The final item, number eighteen, was 'The Battle of the Little Big Horn, Showing with Historical Accuracy the scene of Custer's Last Charge.' On occasion this last item was substituted by 'Attack on a Settler's Cabin – Capture by the Indians – Rescue by "Buffalo Bill" and the Cowboys.'[21]

Cody's initial fame was based upon his exploits as an Indian fighter. And in his entertainments Cody employed the very group of Indians that he had fought with, most of them Sioux drawn from the Pine Ridge reservation in South Dakota. It might seem strange to us that Indians would agree to re-enact scenes dramatizing recent conflicts in which they had, after all, been the losers. (True, Custer had been defeated at the Little Big Horn, but the Indians' triumph was short-lived, and the re-enactment of the event was more about celebrating Custer's romantic heroism than celebrating the Indian victory.) First-hand accounts by Indians themselves of their experience in Cody's show are hard to come by; such comments as are recorded come through interpreters, usually supplied by the shows in which they appeared, who would not have wished unfavourable views to be aired. But to Indians cooped up in the poverty-stricken reservations to which they were now confined, a life on the road with Cody's show, with regular meals and cash money, must have had a strong appeal. Even Sitting Bull, one of the most potent symbols of Indian resistance, who had fled north into Canada after the Little Big Horn to escape American vengeance, was persuaded to tour with the show for a season.

In seizing on the Indians of the northern plains as his protagonists and in dramatizing episodes of the Indian wars, Cody was continuing in the tradition of much nineteenth-century painting and literature, focusing on colourful mounted warriors and seeing Indians only in terms of their conflicts with the whites. Despite one item in the programme devoted to Indian 'life customs', little more than lip-service was paid to Indian culture as something intrinsically interesting and important for its own sake. Cody's whole career, first as a scout for the army and buffalo-hunter for the railroads, then as the subject of dime novels and as performer in stage plays fancifully based on his adventures, scarcely offered him any other perspective. And such a view of Indians was dictated by what the market required. Some people in authority objected to Cody's use of Indians, not because of the potential for humiliation (Sitting Bull was sometimes jeered by the audience, but apparently bore this with dignity). Rather, the government's paternalist view of its Indian charges was incompatible with the potential for freedom that appearing in Cody's entertainment offered. By the late nineteenth century the American government had no legal power to forbid Indians leaving their reservations to seek employment in Wild

West shows. But from 1889 the Commissioner for Indian Affairs, Thomas Jefferson Morgan, did all he could to discourage the practice. The government had its own view of Indians and was determined that it should prevail over others. In Morgan's opinion, the image of Indians that the show presented was detrimental to what had now become the official government policy of assimilation, whereby Indians were to be turned away from their 'primitive' lifestyle and learn how to become whites, forgetting their languages, dress and customs and changing from hunting to farming. Reminding people of what the Indians once were was seen as an obstacle to this project. Morgan stated his objections in a circular:

1. Traveling about the country on such expeditions fosters idleness and a distaste for steady occupation.
2. The Indians are brought in contact with people of low character, and learn the worst habits of the white race.
3. As a result, they frequently return home wrecked morally and physically.[22]

Some Indians were badly treated, but this cannot disguise the deep vein of snobbery and paternalism that underlay the official attitude. Cody went out of his way to demonstrate that his own Indians were well cared for. But he had no intention of altering the manner in which his show represented Indians. Having helped create the demand for screaming mounted savages in war bonnets, he could not afford to disappoint his paying customers.

The huge success of Cody's show was a major factor in fixing a certain image of the Indian in the popular mind. The mounted warrior of the plains, painted, befeathered, wielding his tomahawk or rifle and whooping his war-cry, was so pervasive that it threatened to drive any alternative image from the public imagination. And white heroism came to be defined in relation to this (thankfully now overcome) threat. One episode in Cody's life illustrates the process by which real events become transformed, under the pressure of already established modes of perception, into the raw material of genres. In the summer of 1876 Buffalo Bill was taking time out from his theatrical career, scouting for the US Army. Only a few weeks earlier, on 25 June, General Custer and his Seventh Cavalry had been defeated at the Battle of the Little Big Horn by a combined force of Sioux and Cheyenne. On 17 July the Fifth Cavalry, whom Cody accompanied, surprised a small party of Cheyenne. One was a warrior named Yellow Hair. He wore 'a feathered bonnet, tin bracelets, a charm, a beaded belt wherein was tucked a scalp of yellow or blonde hair, and a breechcloth fashioned from a cotton American flag.' Interestingly, before the encounter Cody, perhaps having a premonition that events might develop in a somewhat theatrical manner, had changed from his usual buckskins into what can only be described as a stage costume, with a red silk shirt, black velvet trousers, a belt with a large, rectangular silver buckle (which in later years he wore when appearing in his show), and a large, floppy beaver-felt hat. Cody and his companions rode towards the Cheyenne. Cody exchanged rifle shots at distance with Yellow Hair.

Cody's first shot killed the Indian's horse, throwing him to the ground. A second shot from Cody killed Yellow Hair, whose companions fled. Dismounting, Cody scalped Yellow Hair, raised the scalp and the feathered bonnet to the air and cried out, 'The first scalp for Custer!'[23]

Cody packed up the trophies he took from Yellow Hair and sent them back to his wife. Later that year Prentiss Ingraham wrote a new play entitled *The Red Right Hand; or, Buffalo Bill's First Scalp for Custer*, in which Cody re-enacted the fight with Yellow Hair. The trophies, including the scalp Cody had taken, were displayed outside the theatre. In his autobiography, published in 1879, Cody related the incident, which was illus-

'The first scalp for Custer', in an untitled watercolour of 1909 by 'Reinhold'.

trated by a woodcut. By now the fight had become a hand-to-hand duel and the Indian's name mysteriously transformed to Yellow Hand. Cody's stance in the woodcut, knife in his right hand, weight on his right foot, the left hand holding the scalp and head-dress aloft, itself appears to be based on a water-colour by the artist Seth Eastman entitled *The Death Whoop* (*c.* 1850), in which a Dakota (Sioux) warrior holds up the scalp of an Ojibwa. So an image of internecine Indian warfare becomes the model for an iconic picture of white triumph over Indians.

The killing and scalping of Yellow Hand (*sic*) subsequently became an item in Cody's Wild West show, and the image of Cody holding up the scalp was included in the printed programme. Subsequently it was recycled in a number of publications, including further editions of Cody's autobiography, and in magazines for boys, before the incident became a scene in *The Indian Wars*, a film that Cody produced in 1913 and which re-enacted several episodes from the Indian wars. Unfortunately the film does not survive, although some stills are extant, including one of the Yellow Hand incident. The image of Cody taking Yellow Hair/Hand's scalp continued to circulate in comics during the twentieth century, and eventually the episode surfaces in a 1952 Hollywood film, *Pony Express*, but with differences. Charlton Heston plays a young Buffalo Bill Cody, who did indeed play a part in the short-lived enterprise of the Pony Express in 1860, though he was only fourteen at the time. In the course of the film, Cody is challenged to a duel by an Indian named Yellow Hand; if Cody wins, the white people whom the Indians have surrounded will be allowed to go free. Cody and Yellow Hand fight it out at close quarters with tomahawks and of course Cody is successful, but there is no scalping. Presumably by this time the audience had become too squeamish for that sort of thing, since scalping was by then perceived as an act performed solely by Indians, or on occasion by renegade whites.

In the process of being transformed from historical fact in 1876 to cinematic representation in 1952, the duel with Yellow Hair loses some of its bloodthirsty and savage edge and is cut loose from its context of revenge for Custer's defeat, while being time-shifted back fifteen years or so. And yet it retains not only its, admittedly by now tenuous, foothold in actual events and the authenticity this supplies to its re-enactment; it also maintains the dramatic force of the original occurrence by expressing the essence of the Western genre, the violent confrontation between civilization and savagery, placing the Indians ineluctably on the side of savagery. Cody was apt to remark of himself, 'I stood between civilization and savagery most all my early days',[24] and the essence of his show was to demonstrate the lesson of recent history. He described the Indians in his autobiography as, 'that savage foe that had been compelled to submit to a conquering civilization and were now accompanying me in friendship, loyalty and peace'. His spectacle was unashamedly intended to reinforce white supremacy, 'intended to prove to the center of the old world civilization that the vast region of the United States was finally and effectively settled by the English-speaking race.'[25]

Photographs of Cody's show do not do justice to the spectacle, at least not to the more action-packed items. At this time photographic equipment was too cumbersome and film speed too slow to record in any detail the staged battles between Indians and cowboys that were the most spectacular parts of the show. Similarly, we have no photographs of action in the Indian wars, only some photographs of the melancholy aftermath, as in the pictures of the Indians slain at the Massacre of Wounded Knee in 1890, which effectively ended all armed Indian resistance.

In any case, photography of Indians in the nineteenth century was apt to imitate what painting had already shown, rather than document a different reality. Photography competed with painting by bringing not a greater sense of realism in terms of fidelity to the conditions of the Indians' actual existence, but only a means of adding a 'reality effect' to images for which a market had already been established. The doyen of all Indian photographers was Edward S. Curtis, who between 1907 and 1930 produced more than forty thousand photographs of Indians, published in a series of volumes entitled *The North American Indian*, heavily subsidized by the millionaire philanthropist J. Pierpont Morgan. Curtis's project was to document Indian life before it disappeared, trampled under foot by the onward march of civilization. He was influenced in this by a group known as the Pictorialists, who were less interested in photography's capacity for recording the world than in its potential for transforming it into something beautiful. In his introduction to his great work, Curtis wrote that 'the fact that the Indian and his surroundings lend themselves to artistic treatment has not been lost sight of.' Nor did he lose sight of the possibilities that photography offered for the manipulation of the image. Curtis had fixed ideas about what it was he was trying to document. As far as he was concerned, there was about his subjects an essential 'Indianness' that he strove to capture. Indians were separate from whites; it was this difference he was after. In so far as Indians had become 'contaminated' through contact with whites, they had ceased to be true Indians. Curtis therefore believed it legitimate to manipulate the image in order to remove any traces of contact with whites and get back to the pristine originals.

Of course by the time he was working there were no Indians left whose lives had not been modified through contact with whites. Indeed, what was the horse but an example of how Indians' lives had been altered by such exchanges? Curtis sometimes felt obliged to supply his subjects with 'authentic' costumes (on occasion even using the same costumes in which to pose Indians from different tribes). He also doctored photographs after they were taken, for example removing the labels that showed Indian tepees made of feed sacks, not the traditional buffalo hide.[26]

Though Curtis's images did enormously extend the range of Indian cultures that were made visible to whites, photographing Indians in virtually every state west of the Mississippi, a haze of nostalgia hangs heavily over his work. Nowhere more so than in his pictures of the plains tribes, about whom an iconography had by now accreted that was almost impossible to ignore. Thus a picture of Sioux Indians entitled *Ogalala War Party*, dating from 1907, shows a group of mounted Indians in war bonnets carrying rifles and spears. Clearly the picture cannot be a documentary record, since by this time the Indian wars had been over for twenty years. Instead, Curtis is trying to show his subjects as they were in their prime, in an idealized state. Many of his pictures of the Sioux and the Cheyenne refer to their subjects as 'warriors' and reconstruct scenes of warfare from the past. The reality of Indian life in the early twentieth century seems to have had little interest for Curtis. What he wished to remember was the time when the Sioux were free to range across the prairies. Yet at the same time as he attempted to recreate it, Curtis acknowledged that

Edward S. Curtis, *Ogalala War Party*, c. 1908.

Edward S. Curtis, *The Vanishing Race – Navaho, c.* 1904.

this past was irretrievable except through the medium of his pictures. Thus a 1904 photograph portrays a group of mounted Navajo riding away from the camera into the desert twilight. His title for this is *The Vanishing Race* and for his caption Curtis wrote: 'The thought which this picture is meant to convey is that the Indians as a race, already shorn of their tribal strength and stripped of their primitive dress, are passing into the darkness of an unknown future.'[27]

Curtis's artistry is not in doubt. Many of his pictures have a genuine emotional power. But that power relies on our having already absorbed the significance contained in the stereotypes he perpetuates. The image of the noble, stoic Indian, dignified in the face of the inevitable decline of his way of life, is one with which we are familiar; its meanings were already in place even before Curtis started his work. A portrait of the Sioux leader Red Cloud, taken by Charles M. Bell in 1880, shows the chief posed against a studio backdrop of painted sky and plasterboard rocks, doubtless to communicate his closeness to the natural world. His elaborate costume of fringed buckskin, porcupine-quill breastplate and single eagle feather mark him as a figure of importance. But it is through his face that the most important meaning of the photograph is communicated. As he stares implacably into the distance, we are forced, through his very lack of expression, to supply the thoughts that run through his mind. And undoubtedly what we read is a noble and stoical acceptance of his fate. Indians are the victims of change, but they themselves do not change.

Not the least refreshing of the ways in which the 1970 film of Thomas Berger's novel *Little Big Man* tried to break with stereotypes was the humour displayed by Old Lodge Skins, memorably played by Chief Dan George. Up till that moment, it seemed as if Indians never laughed, in films or in photographs, despite ample evidence of the role of humour in Indian culture. The melancholic nostalgia that overlays Curtis's photographs was the preferred tone, one adopted by many other photographers working in the early years of the twenti-eth century. Thus Roland Reed (1864–1934) took a series of photographs in which he posed Indians in elaborate tableaux to signal a particular view of the Indian experience. Once

Charles M. Bell,
Red Cloud, 1880.

again, it was based to a great extent on the idea of the Vanishing American, as it had come to be called, the notion that Indians were doomed to disappear, either through assimilation into white society, or, as had already happened to many, through the attrition of warfare and disease. In one picture, *Tribute to the Dead* (1915), two Indians attend a burial platform, their heads bowed in a stance that is suggestive not just of grief but of resignation.

In another Reed picture a line of Indians rides away from the camera towards the mountains. Entitled *Into the Wilderness*

Roland Reed, *Tribute to the Dead*, 1915.

(1915), the picture has an elegiac quality; the title might suggest that Indians and civilization are incompatible. The essential point being communicated is that Indians in their pure, pre-'discovery' state, are doomed. The photograph or painting can preserve a moment, but it cannot arrest the inevitable decline and fall of the Indian way of life. There may well be a connection between the mood being expressed in the pictures (which, it must be remembered, is entirely a construction of whites – Indian photographers had no role to play in this process), and the fact that the end of the nineteenth century marked a low point in Indian fortunes, during which the population of Indians declined to its nadir of 375,000 in 1900, doubtless in part owing to the government policies that were being pursued at the time. Under government initiatives deriving from the Dawes Act of 1887, as we shall see later, Indian reservation land was divided up into individual parcels and some sold off to whites, thus, it was hoped, forcing the Indians to assimilate into white society and so, in effect, ultimately 'vanish'.

The notion of the 'Vanishing American', however, the idea that the Indians were doomed to disappear, already had a long history by this time. As Brian Dippie shows in his detailed study *The Vanishing American: White Attitudes and US Indian Policy*, such predictions can be traced back at least as far as the eighteenth century.[28] By the early nineteenth century they were well established. A writer in 1828 employs metaphors from the natural world to suggest the inevitability,

Roland Reed, *Into the Wilderness*, 1915.

the naturalness, of the Indians' passing: 'We hear the rustling of their footsteps, like that of the withered leaves of autumn, and they are gone for ever. They pass mournfully by us, and they return no more.'[29] Another writer in 1825 puts it thus: 'Slowly and sadly they climb the distant mountains and read their doom in the setting sun. They are shrinking before the mighty tide which is pressing them away; they must soon hear the roar of the last wave, which will settle over them forever.'[30] These statements are contemporaneous with Cooper's similar pronouncements in *The Last of the Mohicans*.

In 1855 Henry Wadsworth Longfellow, a wealthy Harvard professor and a hugely popular poet, published *The Song of Hiawatha*, a long poem whose hypnotic metre (a trochaic tetrameter, for those who care about such things) was based upon the ancient Finnish epic *Kalevala*. Its mythical hero, whose father is the West Wind, is an Ojibway living by the Great Lakes. Hiawatha takes a wife, Minnehaha, from the Dakotah (Sioux) people, and defeats the Corn Spirit, from whose body rises the maize on which his people are to live. But Hiawatha too, despite his legendary strength and wisdom, is fated to fall into a decline. The Indian idyll that he inhabits, one in which the Indians are living in harmony with nature, is interrupted by the arrival of the white men. Hiawatha, it appears, has read the writing on the wall, for despite apparently accepting the presence of the whites, he has seen a darker vision of the future:

> I beheld, too, in that vision
> All the secrets of the future,

Of the distant days that shall be.
I beheld the westward marches
Of the unknown, crowded nations,
All the land was full of people,
Restless, struggling, toiling, striving,
Speaking many tongues, yet feeling
But one heart-beat in their bosoms.
In the woodlands range their axes,
Smoked their towns in all the valleys,
Over all the lakes and rivers
Rushed their great canoes of thunder.
Then a darker, drearier vision
Passed before me, vague and cloud-like.
I beheld our nations scattered,
All forgetful of my counsels,
Weakened, warring with each other;
Saw the remnants of our people
Sweeping westward, wild and woeful,
Like the cloud-rack of a tempest,
Like the withered leaves of Autumn! [31]

Once more, then, the plight of the Indians is likened to a natural event, the passing of the seasons, inevitable, pre-ordained. In so far as any human agency is involved, it is the Indians themselves who have brought on their fate by 'warring' among themselves. Counselling not resistance but acceptance, Hiawatha leaves his people, journeying in his canoe towards the setting sun and oblivion. Longfellow's poem is little read now, even if the name of Hiawatha remains familiar. But in its time it was immensely successful, catching a mood of high-minded respect for the inhabitants of a never-never land before the arrival of the Europeans, while obscuring the fate of their descendants in a rosy-tinted cloud of sentimentality. It was reissued in 1890, illustrated by Frederic Remington, no less, with more than three hundred pen-and-ink sketches in the margins and some twenty black-and-white paintings printed as full-page plates.

Two years after Longfellow published his poem, John Mix Stanley, a prominent painter of Indians, painted a canvas entitled *The Last of Their Race* (1857). It shows a group of Indians by the sea-shore. They sit or stand in an attitude of melancholy resignation, awaiting their fate. At the beginning of the next century such images were still current. James Earle Fraser produced a monumental sculpture for the Panama-Pacific Exposition in San Francisco in 1915; entitled *The End of the Trail*, it shows a solitary Indian on horseback. Both horse and rider have their heads bowed, in an attitude of exhaustion, but also of submission. The warlike warrior of the plains is now reduced to a sad, defeated figure. Fraser's work achieved widespread fame, being reproduced as a paper-weight and on postcards. Two years before, in 1913, Joseph Dixon published a book, *The Vanishing Race*. It was illustrated with photographs taken on a series of expeditions to the west, financed by a wealthy philanthropist, Rodman Wanamaker. The intention, as with Curtis, was to make a record of the Indians because, as the book put it, 'the Indian, as a race, is

James Earle Fraser, *The End of the Trail*, 1915, bronze.

John Mix Stanley,
The Last of Their Race, 1857,
oil on canvas.

fast losing its typical characters and is soon destined to pass completely away.'[32]

In case anyone should miss the point, the pictures had such captions as 'The Final Trail' and 'Vanishing Into the Mists'. One shows a single Indian, mounted on a horse, wearing a feathered head-dress and carrying a feather-tipped lance. He is riding away from the camera into a darkening sky. The photograph is entitled 'The Sunset of a Dying Race'. This concern to document Indian life before it is too late has been labelled 'imperialist nostalgia' by Renato Rosaldo, a tendency by colonialists to regret the passing of cultures that they themselves have destroyed.[33] Employing metaphors of the natural world is, of course, a way of ignoring any possible human agency in the process whereby the Indians have been dispossessed.

Such sentiments eventually found their way into the cinema through the novels of Zane Grey. A dentist from Ohio, who first went west at the age of 35, Grey became an instant convert to the beauty of the south-western landscapes, in which he set a series of phenomenally successful novels published during the 1910s and '20s, most of which were made into movies, often several times over. Grey's novel *The Vanishing American* (1925) has a contemporary setting and tells the story of Nophaie, a Navajo who falls in love with a blonde schoolteacher, Marian. In the version of the story originally published in the *Ladies Home Journal*, Nophaie argues that whites and Indians should intermarry: 'It would make for a more virile race . . . Red blood into white! It means the white race will gain and the Indian vanish.' However, such a solution to the 'problem' of the Indian did not recommend itself to the magazine's readers, who protested vigorously. In consequence, at the publisher's insistence, Grey changed the ending, so that in the book and in the film Nophaie is fatally wounded.[34] The film thus conforms to a pattern of Indian-white romances in the cinema, in which the Indian partner, be they male or female, frequently does not survive the end of the story. Western movies have frequently flirted with the subject of miscegenation: often, as in *Broken Arrow* (1950), *Across the Wide Missouri* (1950), *Distant Drums* (1951), *Little Big Man* (1970), *A Man Called Horse* (1970), *Jeremiah Johnson* (1972), the relationship is destined to end in tragedy, though there are, as we shall see, notable exceptions.

On the last page of *The Vanishing American* Marian watches the Indians riding away into the sunset:

> 'It is – symbolic –' said Marian. 'They are vanishing – vanishing . . . Only a question of swiftly flying time! My Nophaie – the warrior – gone before them! . . . It is well.'
>
> At last only one Indian was left on the darkening horizon – the solitary Shoie – bent in his saddle, a melancholy figure, unreal and strange against that dying sunset – moving on, diminishing, fading, vanishing – vanishing.[35]

The film version contains a curious prologue, set in Monument Valley (over a dozen years before John Ford would

Richard Dix in George B. Seitz's *The Vanishing American* (1925).

turn the location into the iconic Western landscape) and expounding a social Darwinist view of history in which the Navajo are seen conquering the previous occupants of their tribal lands. The implication of the subsequent narrative is inescapable: that the Navajo are themselves destined to be supplanted by a stronger people, the whites.

As we shall see in the next chapter, the cinema offered two main routes towards extinction. In the one the Indian gracefully acknowledges that his time has come and consents to fade from the scene, agreeing to become progressively assimilated into white culture until the last traces of Indian identity have been effaced. In the other, the Indian, almost invariably a mounted warrior of the plains, defiantly fights against the white advance but is inevitably defeated. Either way, his fate is sealed. As Thomas Jefferson Morgan, the Commissioner for Indian Affairs, put it in 1889 in a chilling report to the Secretary of the Interior, 'Indians must conform to "the white man's ways," peaceably if they will, forcibly if they must . . . This civilization may not be the best possible, but it is the best the Indians can get. They cannot escape it, and must either conform to it or be crushed by it.'[36]

However, with rare exceptions, such as the film of Zane Grey's novel, the concept of the Vanishing American was too downbeat and negative on which to base a genre that had aspirations to becoming the mythic expression of popular national consciousness. If the Western was to emerge as the national genre, it needed a foundation more vigorous and virile. The kind of stirring dramatic action that Remington, Buffalo Bill and the dime novels provided offered something altogether more exciting in the depiction of stories in which Indians, far from mournfully declining of their own accord, resisted in a manner that aroused the heroism of their white conquerors.

Thus the Western became established as a genre in which Indians are an essential element in dramatic struggle, though in and of themselves they often have little importance. Their role is to be the obstacle over which the whites must ride. For all this, there was a moment when films were made about Indian life that did not involve conflict with whites and inevitable defeat. In the infancy of American cinema, before the 90-minute feature film evolved, there was a short-lived vogue for stories that presented an idealized view of Indians living a life of picturesque simplicity, in which the narrative motif is often a love story between a young Indian man and woman, or, to use the terms commonly employed in the films, a 'brave' or 'warrior' and a 'maiden'. Typical of such films is *Hiawatha*, produced by the IMP company in 1909. A version of Longfellow's poem, it opens on a scene of a (rather impossibly small) tipi pitched by a river, with woods all around. Hiawatha, played by a white actor manifestly too long in the tooth for the role, makes the elaborate hand and arm gestures the Victorian stage tradition had deemed appropriate to Indians. In a series of static tableaux (the camera never moves) we witness him court Minnehaha and fight with his father Mudjekeewis. The Indians wear the typical costumes of plains Indians (buckskins, feathered bonnets) but, as in the poem, what is intended is a woodland culture and there are no horses as there would be on the plains. The lush meadows, the rivers and trees differ from the type of landscape that later came to be associated with the Western, since at this time most Westerns were still being shot in the eastern United States, not in the arid south-west.

In D. W. Griffith's early Westerns the Indian is frequently the hero: Angela Aleiss has calculated that, in his thirty Indian-themed films, the Indian was the villain in only eight. Even when Indians attack, they often do so because they are provoked. *Comata the Sioux* (1909) was advertised with the question: 'If [the Indian] has been guilty of any lawlessness, it has been induced by his misanthropic attitude towards the white man, and can we blame him?'[37] Griffith's first film with an Indian as the central character is *The Redman and the Child* (1908), in which a lone Indian is faced with the increasing incursions of white miners in Colorado. The Indian is friendly with a young white boy and his grandfather and when two white criminals, intent on finding the gold that the Indian has discovered, murder the grandfather and take the boy hostage, the Indian strips off his civilized clothes and gives chase, killing the two men and rescuing the boy. In *The Mended Lute* (1909), subtitled 'A Stirring Romance in the Dakotas', Griffith tells a story that, like *Hiawatha*, is set among the Indians before the arrival of the whites. It's a romance between Little Bear (Owen Moore) and Rising Moon (Florence Lawrence). Little Bear has to run for his life when threatened by another of Rising Moon's suitors, Standing Rock (James Kirkwood), though eventually he reaches safety. Publicity material made great play with the film's authenticity in the matter of costumes and dances; although it was shot in Cuddebackville, New York, and the main parts are played by white actors, the film also features James Young Deer and his wife Red Wing, who were to play important roles in the creation of early Indian Westerns.

Filmed at the same time, Griffith's *The Indian Runner's Romance* (1909) used identical casts, costumes and location, and shows a similar interest in Indian ethnography, with the depiction of wedding customs as Blue Cloud (Owen Moore) takes a wife (Mary Pickford). Blue Cloud has learned the location of a mining claim and his wife is kidnapped in order to force him to reveal the whereabouts of the claim, but he rescues her and returns safely. *The Song of the Wildwood Flute* (1910), another Griffith film, is once again set in an Indian world into which whites have not yet intruded. Gray Cloud (played by Dark Cloud, an actor with Indian ancestry whose real name was Elijah Tahamont)[38] woos Dove Eyes (Mary Pickford) by means of a traditional flute. They marry, but a jealous rival imprisons Gray Cloud in a deep bear-pit. Dove Eyes pines away, despite the attentions of a medicine man, until, taking pity on her, the rival rescues Gray Cloud and returns him to his true love. Again, the Indians are in plains costume, but living in tipis in idyllic woodland surroundings, with no horses evident.

A still from D. W. Griffith's *The Song of the Wildwood Flute* (1910).

Griffith's *The Redman's View* (1909) offers another idealized version of Indian life, though this time disrupted by the intrusion of whites. Silver Eagle (Owen Moore) and Minnewanna (no casting information is given) are married, but white men force them off their land and enslave Minnewanna. The tribe are forced to trek westward in search of new lands. Silver Eagle at last rescues her, and in the last scene the couple are paying their respect at the bier of Silver Eagle's father. The figure of the Vanishing American is powerfully present here; as a result of the harsh treatment by whites, the Indians seem doomed to wander ceaselessly in search of refuge.

Inter-racial romances occur in several of Griffith's films. In *The Chief's Daughter* (1911) a white man seduces an Indian girl, only for her to be decisively rejected by white society and forced to return to her people. In *Heredity* (1912) a white renegade has purchased an Indian bride, but when their son is born 'racial difference between father and son is felt',[39] and eventually the mother and child return to the tribe. Griffith's animosity to the idea of sexual relationships between whites and blacks is most notoriously expressed in his epic *Birth of a Nation* (1915); relations between Indians and whites seem not to have aroused the same feelings of disgust, but ultimately, it is clear, Griffith sees them as doomed.

According to Richard Abel, half of all Westerns made between 1907 and 1910 featured Indians.[40] Some are all-Indian stories, in others the Indians are often helpful to whites, as if, at the moment when Indians appeared to be 'vanishing', whites could afford to see their 'good' side, even showing

Indians as morally superior, exhibiting the values of loyalty, self-sacrifice and constancy in love befitting the concept of the noble savage, contrasted with the venality of whites. The savagery so often ascribed to Indians is transferred in some of these early films, so that it is the whites who require a civilizing hand. In an Essanay film, *The Indian Maiden's Lesson* (1911), two miners are prospecting. When they discover gold one attacks the other, leaving him for dead. He is found by an Indian girl on horseback (the scenery this time is more authentically 'Western'). Other Indians arrive and stand looking, their arms crossed on their chests in the approved dramatic stance. The wounded man recovers and teaches the girl to read, writing 'Thou shalt not kill' on a slate as part of the lesson. When his partner is captured by the tribe, the white man wants to avenge himself by stabbing him to death, but the Indian maiden holds up the slate as an admonition.

In a Pathé film of 1910, *White Fawn's Devotion*, a white settler is informed he has inherited a fortune and must leave his Indian wife to collect it. Distraught by grief at his departure, she tries to stab herself. Their child, believing her father has killed her mother, rushes off to her tribe to enlist their help. They capture the white man, but he is saved from death by his devoted wife, happily recovered. It might be that the woodland setting, despite once again putting the actors in plains Indian costumes, is the result of the film being made in the east, but it is in keeping with the 'Hiawatha' mode in which Indians live in close proximity to a benevolent nature corresponding to European notions of the pastoral.

White Fawn's Devotion was directed by James Young Deer, a very rare example of an Indian director working in the mainstream film industry. The publicity for the film claimed that the Indians are played by genuine Native Americans, although in terms of setting, costumes and such the film is not noticeably more 'authentic' than others of the time, generic constraints proving stronger than the urge towards realism. Young Deer was a Winnebago Indian, as was his wife, Lillian Red Wing (born Lillian St Cyr). Red Wing became a star, to the extent that her name is used in the title of some of her films, as in *The Flight of Red Wing*, produced in 1910 by the Bison company, which at the time was making three types of Indian picture: the 'squaw man' plot, about a white settler married to an Indian woman (usually with tragic consequences), the 'good' Indian who helps white people and is befriended by them, and the all-Indian tale of romance and rivalry.[41] In *The Flight of Red Wing*, an example of the second type, Red Wing is courted by an unappealing Indian suitor. Her father insists she must marry him and so she flees. She is rescued by a cowboy. When the Indians attack, the cowboys fight them off, leaving Red Wing with her new-found white suitor.

Young Deer's films about mixed-race couples aroused controversy at the time (in its review, *Moving Picture World* even said of one film that it aroused 'a feeling of disgust'),[42] and his later films moved away from such challenging material.[43] The popularity of this sub-genre, showing idealized Indians in a pastoral setting, coincides with the nostalgia expressed by Curtis and other photographers of the period, one in which the actual threat posed by Indians had been overcome and Indian populations were at their lowest ebb since the arrival of Columbus. It is as if, now that Indians were on the wane, whites could afford to indulge themselves with comforting stories showing the attractions of their way of life. But this era was short-lived. Before long such idyllic visions had largely been supplanted by stories in which Indians are an obstacle in the way of white expansion, one that must be removed by force if necessary.

Scott Simmon has argued that this change is the result of the switch in locations, from the leafy environs of upper New York State, where Griffith's and other early Westerns were shot, to the more arid conditions of California. Although some production continued in the east, California soon became the centre of gravity of the American film industry, its climate offering perfect conditions for outdoor filming, and the border with Mexico providing a convenient escape route for those being pursued for patents evasion by the monopolizing Motion Picture Patents Company.[44] In Simmon's view, the more open landscapes of the west led to an abandonment of the pastoral mode, and the embrace of a conflict model, in which the white and the red contended for the occupation of the empty spaces of the prairie and desert. For this kind of story the inspiration was less Longfellow and Cooper, and more the violent encounters enacted on the canvases of Remington and in the arena of Buffalo Bill's Wild West.

The change is marked in Griffith's films once he moved his productions west. In *Fighting Blood* (1911), shot in the San Fernando Valley outside Los Angeles, an isolated settler defends his log cabin against attacks by the Sioux. In *The Last Drop of Water* (1911), a wagon train, marooned in the desert by Indian attacks, is saved by the cavalry. *The Battle at Elderbush Gulch* (1913), Griffith's most ambitious Western to date, presents the Indians as unremittingly savage and hostile, eaters of dogs and murderers of children, who besiege white women and children until the cavalry ride to the rescue.

Griffith's films were matched in terms of scope and scale by those of Thomas Ince, who had gone west in 1911 to take over production of Westerns for the New York Motion Picture Company. Ince's coup was in securing the services of the Miller Brothers 101 Ranch show, a rival to Buffalo Bill's, which was touring in California. Ince thereby acquired not only a collection of props and costumes suitable for making Westerns, he also contracted with the company's band of Oglala Sioux, who were put to work in a series of films such as *War on the Plains* (1912),

A still from D. W. Griffith's *The Battle at Elderbush Gulch* (1913).

The Inceville Sioux in *Custer's Last Fight* (1912).

Custer's Last Fight (1912) and *The Invaders* (1912). Altogether Ince filmed around eighty dramas with the Sioux, who originated from the Pine Ridge Reservation in South Dakota. Because they were legally wards of the federal government, Ince need official sanction for his contract with them.

In *The Invaders* conflict is generated between the Sioux and the army when surveyors for the coming railroad intrude upon Indian lands. Superimposed on this historical material is a pair of romances, one between the daughter of the commander at the fort and a young officer, the other between the Indian chief's daughter, Sky Star, and a surveyor; though mortally injured, Sky Star saves the day by alerting the fort to an impending Indian attack, before gracefully expiring. Ince's Bison 101 films, as they were branded, were produced at a ranch near Santa Monica, soon dubbed 'Inceville'. The Inceville Sioux, prominent among them William Eagleshirt, undoubtedly lent authenticity to these films, as well as consolidating in the public's mind the notion that the essential Indian was one who rode a horse, wielded a tomahawk or bow and arrow and wore feathers in his hair and deerskin leggings. It was, of course, chiefly Sioux who were employed by Buffalo Bill. But such a close identification between the Sioux (and to some extent Cheyenne) and the Indians represented in popular entertainment had already been forged during the Plains Wars of the 1860s and '70s, which were the subject of intense interest in the popular press at the time and which now provided the historical backdrop for the films of Ince, Griffith and many others.

Simmon's argument that the change from idyllic to warlike Indian was motivated by the switch in location from

The Inceville Sioux with William S. Hart and Thomas Ince.

east to west perhaps places an overly heavy burden on the effects of landscape. Other forces may have been involved. By 1912 it was apparent that cinema was a mass medium that put a premium upon physical action and romance. The innocence and charm of the pastoral Indian films may simply have been outperformed at the box office by tales of derring-do. The literary credentials of the pastoral Indian films meant little to the working-class, often immigrant, audience who went en masse to the cinema. And romance involving Indians, whether among themselves or across the racial divide, appeared to be increasingly problematic, as James Young Deer discovered.

Causation in film history is always a difficult question. Social and historical forces can never be discounted, but it is not always easy to assess what weight to give them, or to perceive the mechanism whereby their effectiveness is achieved. So often film production goes in cycles, following trends until they are played out and the next one comes along. The trade press was full of articles at this period forecasting the imminent demise of the Western, and such prophecies may have been self-fulfilling, at least in respect of the pastoral cycle. What is certain is that by 1920 Indian subjects were few and far between. In the 'epic' Westerns of the mid-1920s, such as *The Covered Wagon* (1923) and *The Iron Horse* (1924), Indians feature merely as one of the hazards of westward expansion overcome by the whites. True, there were occasional films based on prestigious literary works that attempted a more nuanced or sympathetic view. Back in 1914 Cecil B. DeMille had made a film of Edwin Milton Royle's successful

Cecil B. DeMille (left) with his company filming *The Squaw Man* (1914).

play *The Squaw Man*, premiered in 1905. The film has a claim to be the first feature-length film produced within the environs of Hollywood. It is also another episode in the parade of tragic interracial romances. An English aristocrat comes out to Wyoming to escape a scandal at home. He marries an Indian girl, who proves her savage origins by killing her husband's white enemy. The Englishman decides his son must be educated back home. The distraught wife, bereft of her child and fearing the law will catch up with her, commits suicide, thus opening the way for the aristocrat's white fiancée to arrive with the good news that the scandal is resolved and she may now marry him. DeMille liked the material so much that he filmed it again in 1918 and once more in 1931.

Other literary adaptations of the silent period included *The Last of the Mohicans* (1920; D. W. Griffith had produced his own version, *Leatherstocking*, in 1909) and Helen Hunt Jackson's 1884 interracial romance *Ramona* (1928; again, Griffith had directed a version in 1910). Both these stories present 'good' Indians for our admiration. There was also the significant, if short-lived, phenomenon of a small group of films about the Indian in modern-day America. These for the most part present the same situation as that in *The Vanishing American*. In *Braveheart* (1925), Rod La Roque plays a young Indian who attends a white college. In consequence his tribe reject him. He begins a relationship with a white woman, but eventually renounces white society and returns to his tribe to help fight for their fishing rights. In *Redskin* (1929) Richard Dix, also the star of *The Vanishing American*, plays a Navajo athlete who finds himself between two worlds when he attends a white college, where he is tolerated only for his physical abilities. Although he is attractive to white women, he eventually returns to his roots and marries a Pueblo Indian girl. The implications are clear: intermarriage is fraught with problems.

In 1934 Warner Bros, consistent with its efforts to support the New Deal of Franklin D. Roosevelt, produced *Massacre* (1934), in which Richard Barthelmess plays a contemporary Sioux who travels to Washington to alert the government to the wrongs being done to Indians on the reservation. Apart from this, Hollywood in the 1930s showed scant interest in dealing with Indians as a serious subject for drama.

Most of the Westerns produced during this decade were B-features, cheaply made on Poverty Row and designed for the bottom half of a double bill. These films had little time, either literally (they usually ran under an hour in length) or figuratively, for the issues raised by 'the Indian question'.

John Ford's *Stagecoach* (1939), although produced for a major studio (United Artists) and partly responsible through its box-office success for the revival of the A-feature Western at the end of the 1930s, has much in common with the B-Westerns that its star, John Wayne, had been making throughout the decade. Like many cheaper films, it views Indians as essentially an obstacle to be overcome in the onward march of civilization. At the beginning of the film we learn that Geronimo is on the warpath, but he never appears as a character in the film. When the Apache leader's name is mentioned, striking fear into those who hear it, we cut to a close-up of an unnamed Indian staring at the camera, lit from below to give him a menacing appearance. Though a soldier says that 'He's a Cheyenne, they hate Apaches worse than we do', the effect is anything but reassuring. When later the Apaches appear and launch their attack on the stagecoach, none of them is identified. They are presented en masse, appearing suddenly out of the landscape, a force of nature not characters in the drama.

Much the same could be said of Ford's first colour film, *Drums along the Mohawk* (1939), set during the American War of Independence. This time an Indian does appear as a character. Chief Big Tree plays Blue Back, who pops up out of nowhere on a dark night to give the heroine, Claudette Colbert,

'He's a Cheyenne . . .': Chief Big Tree as the anonymous Indian in John Ford's *Stagecoach* (1939).

the fright of her life. Her husband, played by Henry Fonda, laughingly explains that the Indian is his trusted servant, but as in *Stagecoach* the intended reassurance comes only after we, the audience, have had our prejudices confirmed. And when Indians appear later, they are conceived much as in *Stagecoach*, an anonymous, undifferentiated band of hostiles, whether attacking the settlers' fort or chasing Henry Fonda through the woods. They play no role as protagonists in the drama; instead they are simply a weapon used by the unscrupulous British in their war against the American revolutionaries.

Portraying Indians as mere impediments to the triumph of Manifest Destiny, the god-given right of whites to overrun the continent, was a habit that continued into the next decade. Though Ford was ultimately to change his view of Indians, this did not come about as a sudden conversion on the road to Damascus. Rather, it appears to have been more of a two steps forward, one step back process. In the first two

films of his so-called cavalry trilogy, *Fort Apache* (1948) and
She Wore a Yellow Ribbon (1949), he is generally more sympathetic: Indians have speaking roles and conflict is either the
fault of white prejudice or young hotheads, not inherent in
the Indians' nature. But the last film of the trilogy, *Rio Grande*
(1950), is a throwback to the earlier position. Apaches have
kidnapped white children and clearly intend to kill them,
until the children are rescued by John Wayne and the cavalry.
Officials of the Production Code, Hollywood's self-regulatory
body, criticized the script, insisting that 'it behoves the industry to see to it that Indians in Motion Pictures are fairly
presented.' They objected in particular to lines such as 'These
Apaches are the only Indians who kill and torture for the
sheer lust of it.' But though the line was subsequently taken
out, the Apaches rape and murder a soldier's wife, and there is
no attempt to humanize them.[45]

But demonizing the Apache was not the only offence of
which Hollywood can be accused during the 1930s and '40s.
Three films directed by Cecil B. DeMille are guilty of worse.
In *The Plainsman* (1936) Gary Cooper plays Wild Bill Hickok
and Jean Arthur is Calamity Jane. Captured by the Sioux,
Calamity calls them 'painted buzzards', 'red hyenas'. Speaking
very slowly in deep voices, in the stereotypical 'me heep big
chief' style that Hollywood employed to represent racial
difference, the Indians soon reveal themselves as simple-
minded, Hickok managing to negotiate Calamity's return by
exchanging her for a chiming watch that appeals to the Indians'
childlike nature. Later the Indians reveal their savagery as

Hickok is roasted over an open fire in an attempt to persuade him to reveal the location of the cavalry under General Custer.

In DeMille's next Western, *Union Pacific* (1939), Indians hold up a train in which the white heroine (Barbara Stanwyck) is travelling across the plains. These 'red devils', as she describes them, loot the contents, deriving childish pleasure from firing arrows into a piano and capturing a wooden Indian, which they appear to regard as a religious object. One of the Indians discovers a lady's corset and attempts to wrap it round his horse as a decoration. These antics are clearly intended to arouse derisive laughter in the audience. When rescuers arrive on another train the Indians are soon routed.

In *Unconquered* (1947) Indians are once again simpletons, easily duped by the whites. They are treacherous too: the film is set during the Seven Years War, and in league with the French the Indians commit a series of massacres upon white American settlers by offering them safe passage under a white flag, then falling upon them after they surrender. Paulette Goddard is captured and stripped to her underwear before being tied to the stake. 'I've heard what they do to white women,' she has said earlier, thus preparing us for 'the fate worse than death'. Threatened with red-hot spears and eagle's claws covered in burning pitch, she cowers in terror. 'White woman burn,' intones Boris Karloff as the Indian chief. But Gary Cooper strides into the Indians' camp, throwing a handful of gunpowder into the fire to impress them with his 'magic'. He persuades the gullible Indians that a compass needle obeys his command to turn in any way he wishes; by the time the Indians have puzzled out the trick he and Goddard have made good their escape.

This combination of simple-mindedness and savagery is the dominant image of Indians in the 1930s, but early in the next decade come signs of a change of attitude. In *They Died with their Boots On* (1941), George Armstrong Custer is portrayed as generally well disposed towards the Indians. All the trouble is caused by Machiavellian businessmen seeking to exploit Indian lands; by contrast, on the eve of the fateful Battle of the Little Big Horn Custer has a discussion with a British officer in his command, who remarks, to Custer's evident approval, that 'the only real Americans in this merry old parish are on the other side of the hill with feathers in their hair.' As we shall see in the next chapter, some of the implications of this remark are explored in the 1950s, when, after a world war fought in part to combat racism, and in which Indians had given distinguished service in the American military, there was a concerted effort by Hollywood to redress the balance of racism in its depiction of the Indian.

2 the liberal western

Since its appearance in 1950, *Broken Arrow* has been widely regarded as a breakthrough in the representation of the Indian on the screen, and regularly cited as a milestone on Hollywood's road towards a more liberal view of Indian-white relations. Set in 1870, the story is recounted in a voice-over by the principal character, Tom Jeffords (James Stewart), an army scout. Based to an extent on historical fact, the film explores the relationship between the Chiricuahua Apache, under their chief Cochise, and the United States army charged with the pacification of the Indians. Initially no different in his attitude towards the Indians from any other white, Jeffords is treated with respect by the Apache when he commits an act of kindness towards an injured Apache boy, and comes to feel friendship for them. Eventually he courts and marries a beautiful Apache woman, with the blessing of Cochise. Shortly after their marriage she is killed by hostile whites, but the peace that Jeffords has negotiated with Cochise holds.

Despite the fact that Cochise and the Apache woman Sonseeahray are played by white actors (Jeff Chandler and Debra Paget), the film makes some effort to portray Apache culture. The opening credits are over images of Indian paintings on deerskin. Having decided to attempt a peace overture

Delmer Daves's *Broken Arrow* (1950): Sonseeahray (Debra Paget) in her wedding dress, with Tom Jeffords (James Stewart), Cochise (Jeff Chandler) and Nalikadeya (Argentina Brunetti).

to Cochise, Jeffords makes a determined effort to learn Apache customs and their language (although the film does not go so far as to show us the Apache speaking their own language). On his first visit to Cochise's camp, which consists of ethnographically correct wood and grass wickiups, not the tipis Indians usually inhabit on-screen, Jeffords observes a ritual dance and Cochise explains its cultural significance as a puberty ceremony.

The film's argument in favour of reconciliation is carefully constructed. Jeffords begins as a racist, like most of the whites in the film, but is quickly if simplistically won over to the view that the Apaches are human beings too when the boy he has rescued explains that his mother will be crying at the thought that he is lost. In an argument back in town Jeffords resists the notion that the Apaches have started the conflict, recalling massacres of Apache women and children by whites, and the murder of Cochise's brother under a flag of truce. Fired up by the hostility of the whites to the Apache, Jeffords is provoked into a truly radical remark: 'Who asked us [i.e. the whites] here in the first place?' The implications of this are not fully pursued, since the film does not elsewhere challenge the rights of the whites to be in Apache territory. Instead, it falls back on the position that violence between whites and Indians is caused not by irreconcilable differences but by the actions of bad people on both sides. Given proper understanding, and an acceptance by the Indians that change in their traditional way of life is inevitable, peaceful coexistence can be achieved.

The film's liberalism undoubtedly owes something to its screenwriter. Based on *Blood Brother*, a novel by Elliott Arnold, the film was initially credited to Michael Blankfort, since its actual writer, Albert Maltz, was one of the original Hollywood Ten who had been labelled unfriendly witnesses by the House Un-American Activities Committee in 1947 and subsequently blacklisted by the studios. Maltz had joined the Communist Party in 1935, together with many writers and other intellectuals, and drew inspiration from its anti-racist stance. However, the political position that the film puts forward is not a Marxist analysis but one whose ostensible liberalism is based on attitudes ingrained in the institutional history of relations between Indians and whites going back at least a century before the film was made. Without a knowledge of such history, the film remains perfectly coherent, but all too easily classified merely as the simple humanist document it aspires to be.

From the beginning of European incursions into America, Indians were seen by white settlers as a 'problem'. The source of conflict was plain enough. Indians occupied land that was coveted by the whites, and were usually willing to fight to defend it. After independence from Britain, the official policy of the United States was to treat the Indians as autonomous nations, with which the government agreed a series of treaties. Even though the Indians negotiated under duress and promises were often broken, the US government maintained its stance that such treaties were binding when they handed Indian lands over to the possession of the whites.

By the 1820s government policy was hardening. Co-existence was deemed no longer possible: Indians could not live cheek by jowl with whites and could only preserve their autonomy if they agreed to be removed to lands further west, far away from white settlement. Accordingly the so-called Five Civilized Tribes (Choctaw, Chickasaw, Creek, Cherokee and Seminole, whose ancestral lands were in the south-east), were forcibly removed to lands west of the Mississippi. As the whites expanded, however, they put pressure on Indians further west. The original notion that there might be a substantial portion of the continent permanently under Indian sovereignty was abandoned in favour of a new policy, formalized in 1853, under which Indians would be confined to designated areas or reservations.

Although there was continuous debate during the nineteenth century between those who simply wanted the Indians got rid of and those who, usually on Christian principles, argued for a humane policy, there was a high degree of unanimity that the Indians in their original state were in any case eventually destined to fade away. As Brian Dippie shows in *The Vanishing American*, his comprehensive survey of white attitudes and policy towards the Indians, there was virtual unanimity among whites throughout the nineteenth century that Indians were doomed to extinction. As we saw in the previous chapter, a series of metaphors from the natural world were invoked to express this inevitable fate. Indians would be blown away like autumn leaves, or would melt like 'April snow'. In 1825 Charles Sprague, a Boston banker, declared in a speech: 'Slowly and sadly they climb the distant mountains, and read their doom in the setting sun. They are shrinking before the mighty tide which is pressing them away . . . '.[1]

To some, this prediction of Indian extinction was based on simple racism, a view that the Indians were so inferior that they could not possibly compete with whites. Whether their decline stemmed from an inherent tendency to drunkenness or disease, or an unwillingness to work, they simply could not maintain themselves against white superiority. There were even suggestions that their sexual potency was low compared to whites. A more benevolent view, which gained strength as Darwinian ideas about evolution began to be applied within the social sciences as well as the biological, was that human civilization advanced to maturity in the same manner as an individual, and thus Indian development was still at the stage of childhood. In consequence, Indians had a right to be looked after, but could not be given responsibility for their own affairs. Although such a view did not treat Indians as innately inferior, and held out the possibility of future development, it assumed that there was only one route towards civilization, the characteristics of which followed the model of the Christianized west. It allowed for no thoughts of multiculturalism or pluralism, of alternative social models.[2]

If Indians were at an early, childlike state of development, they needed to be wards of the government until such time as they could achieve maturity and self-government. While for some the reservation system was a means of herding Indians together so they could be kept an eye on, for those who saw themselves as reformers the reservation was a system in which Indians could be protected from white competition while they were led upwards to a higher form of life.

For the reformers the ultimate goal was to integrate Indians into white society. Indians would vanish by becoming invisible through assimilation. There were four essentials to be inculcated if this was to be achieved. First, Indians must be turned from nomads to farmers. The idea of the yeoman farmer had long been a cornerstone of American political ideology, most memorably formulated by Thomas Jefferson.

Agriculture was held to be the foundation of both a sound economy and of civic virtue. Honest toil on the land would make Indians into honest citizens. Secondly, Indians must be educated. Thus arose the notorious Carlisle School and its imitators, designed to take Indian children away from their parents and indoctrinate them into white culture, even to the extent of forbidding them the use of their own language. Thirdly, the Indians must be Christianized and their own 'heathen' religions rooted out, by force if necessary. Lastly, the notion of the communal ownership of land, a widespread principle in Indian societies, must be eliminated. Only private property could provide sufficient incentive to work hard and get ahead. As one nineteenth-century commentator put it: 'The Indian will never be reclaimed until he ceases to be a communist. He will be a vagabond and a pauper so long as he is not an individual proprietor and possessor.'[3]

By the 1870s assimilation had become overwhelmingly the aim of white policy towards the Indians. Confining Indians to reservations was a temporary measure until Indians could be forced to divest themselves of their culture and become individual proprietors working the land. In 1887 Congress decided that this moment had come and passed the Dawes Severalty Act, which instituted the policy of 'allotment' whereby the Indian lands within reservations were to be divided up into 160-acre plots and distributed among individual Indian families, who would eventually be free to dispose of them as they chose. All the land left over after each family was awarded its plot was then available for sale to whites. In this way tribal structures would be weakened and communal ways of life undermined. The result was that, whereas at the time of the Act's passing 138 million acres were in Indian hands, by 1934, when legislation under Roosevelt's New Deal stopped the policy of allotment, two-thirds of this land had passed into white hands.[4]

Under these policies, Indian social and family structures, culture and belief systems were intended to wither away, and Indians, apart possibly from some vestigial physical characteristics, were to be indistinguishable from whites. They would vanish into the melting pot of American society. This then was the official view of the Indian future in the 1870s when *Broken Arrow* is set. The Apache, as an army general explains, are to be herded onto reservations and given the tools to become farmers. However, there is another context for the film that needs to be taken into account. Although under the New Deal the policy of allotment was reversed and, under the direction of John Collier, President Roosevelt's Indian Commissioner, efforts were made to strengthen tribal societies with programmes to improve their physical and cultural health, after the Second World War there was yet another change in policy, towards what was called 'termination'. In effect this meant the government progressively withdrawing from any further involvement in Indian affairs, so that Indians would cease to have any special legal status. Assimilation was assumed to be, if not yet quite achieved, then just around the corner.

Steve Neale, citing other critics such as Frank Manchel and Angela Aleiss, has argued that *Broken Arrow* endorses the policy of termination.[5] This is surely a mis-reading. The whole tendency of the film's argument is towards the continuing engagement of the white authorities in shepherding the Indians towards eventual integration. This should by no means be confused with the unseemly rush to leave the Indians to their own devices (thus saving federal funds), which Republican administrations favoured in the 1950s and which was dignified with the label of 'termination'.[6] *Broken Arrow* in fact mounts powerful arguments in favour of the reservation system as a humane solution to the Indian 'problem'. This is what gives the film its liberal credentials, and this liberalism, a form of benevolent paternalism, would have seemed all the more pointed in the early 1950s, at a time when pressure from conservatives in Washington was building for the government to get out of the 'Indian business' altogether and leave Indians to their own devices, to sink or swim.

The crucial scene in the film's political project comes towards the end. Having established his position as trusted go-between by his desire to marry into the tribe, Jeffords agrees to conduct General Howard to a meeting with Cochise. Like Jeffords and Cochise themselves, Oliver Otis Howard is a historical character, popularly known as 'the Christian General', who had lost an arm in the Civil War but gained a reputation for moral courage and probity. His Christian principles and anti-racist views are established in his remark to Jeffords that 'My bible says nothing about the pigmentation of the skin.' Howard tells Cochise that the Apache may no longer raid against the Mexicans. Instead, they will be given livestock and expected to farm. This is rejected by one of the Apache leaders, Geronimo, played by the Indian actor Jay Silverheels.[7]

Geronimo is presented as a scowling and aggressive character, implacably hostile to whites. He has already appeared in earlier scenes, and when Jeffords is captured at the start of the film Geronimo is all for killing him. He rejects Howard's offer: 'It is not the Apache way to be grandmothers to cattle.' Cochise, he says, is a woman, cowardly to even consider it. But Cochise has his arguments well thought-out. Earlier Jeffords has told him that the Apache are few and the whites many. In other words, history is not on his side. Now Cochise counters Geronimo:

> The Americans keep cattle, but they are not soft or weak. Why should not the Apache be able to learn new ways? It is not easy to change but sometimes it is required. The Americans are growing stronger while we are growing weaker. If a big wind comes, a tree must bend, or be lifted out by its roots.

Cochise is a realist. One must face facts. The peace offer is put to the vote. Geronimo rejects it, walking away with half a dozen other leaders. But the great majority remain on Cochise's side. In a voice of near-despair, seeing himself isolated, Geronimo entreats others to join him. 'Who else comes? Who else?' There are none. Geronimo, having chosen the way of rejection, of continued violence against hopeless odds, is doomed. And doomed with him is the possibility of

Indians preserving their culture in its original form. Looking back from the 1950s, the film argues for the logic of history. That the Apache would not be able to continue with their way of life unchecked, including their custom of raiding for livestock, is inevitable given the irresistible flow of westward immigration by whites. Geronimo's is a lost cause, and his recalcitrance will end only in his defeat.

In films of this period Geronimo is consistently portrayed as implacably hostile, one who refuses to see the logic of assimilation. *The Battle at Apache Pass* (1952), though made after *Broken Arrow*, is a kind of prequel, set during the Civil War, a decade earlier. Cochise and Geronimo are played by the same two actors, Jeff Chandler and Jay Silverheels, the one a white actor, handsome and charming, the other a Native American, thickset, with coarse, fleshy features and a guttural voice. It's not hard to guess whom the white audience is supposed to identify with. Once again the two are enemies,

Jay Silverheels as Geronimo and Jeff Chandler as Cochise in George Sherman's *The Battle at Apache Pass* (1952).

Geronimo accusing Cochise at the beginning of being a friend of the Americans. Whereas Cochise is here seen in a domestic situation (his wife is pregnant and he is concerned for her welfare, as well as being responsible for the upbringing of his younger brother), Geronimo is a loner (in fact he had several wives). Through the machinations of a wily civilian adviser to the army, Geronimo is induced to break the peace and Cochise's Chiricahua are blamed for it. In an incident based on historical fact, Cochise is captured with some other Apaches, but escapes by cutting through the side of a tent. He too becomes hostile and joins forces with Geronimo: 'Now the enemies of Geronimo are the enemies of Cochise.' During the culminating battle that gives the film its title, the army turns its howitzers on the Indians and Cochise sues for peace, once more provoking Geronimo to break with him. The two men fight and Geronimo is beaten and forced into exile. As usual in films of a liberal bent, war has been caused by bad men on both sides, not by any inherent conflict between the Indians and the whites. Cochise, showing goodwill and a willingness to compromise, is able to restore peace.

From his first appearance in a sound film, in John Ford's *Stagecoach* (1939), where he is never more than a shadowy presence yet every white settler's nightmare, Geronimo more than any other historical figure came to represent the intractable, rejectionist Indian. In another 1950s film, *Walk the Proud Land* (1956), a Universal-International production like *Broken Arrow* and *The Battle at Apache Pass*, Geronimo (once more played by Jay Silverheels) turns up on the San

John Clum with the Apaches Diablo and Eskiminzin in 1875.

Carlos reservation where agent John Clum (a historical figure played by Audie Murphy) is bringing enlightened management. Geronimo is interested only in recruiting warriors to fight the whites. In U-I's sequel to *Broken Arrow*, *Taza, Son of Cochise* (1954), Geronimo (this time played by a white actor, Ian MacDonald, who in looks is no match for the handsome Rock Hudson, playing Taza) is once more the rallying point for those who reject an accommodation with the whites. The film begins with the death of Cochise, and Geronimo, though in a minor role, predictably uses this as an opportunity to reignite the flames of war.

In the 1962 film *Geronimo* the title role is again taken by a white actor, but this time he is a star, Chuck Connors, a clear signal that a more sympathetic treatment is being considered. At the beginning of the film Geronimo is recalcitrant. Having agreed to surrender, but only on his terms, he despises the reservation Apaches who are growing corn, dismissing it as women's work. (In *Apache*, 1954, Massai [Burt Lancaster] also rejects the notion of growing corn as unworthy, but eventually relents and plants the seeds given him by a Cherokee who has chosen the white man's way.) When the corrupt Indian agent starts selling off the land the Apache have been working, Geronimo leads a mass break-out. Although his band becomes progressively depleted and is running out of food and ammunition, he refuses to surrender. This time, however, Geronimo has a partner, Teela, a beautiful Apache woman (played by Kamala Devi, an Indian of a different kind, born in Bombay). She gives birth to his son in the middle of an attack by the

Burt Lancaster and a handful of corn in Robert Aldrich's *Apache* (1954).

Geronimo at the wheel in Oklahoma in 1905.

army, and a new-found sense of his domestic responsibilities finally persuades Geronimo to surrender, after a US Senator sent by President Cleveland has promised the Apaches respect and dignity. (In fact, after his surrender Geronimo was held in captivity, first in Florida, then in Oklahoma.) Thus the price Geronimo as a film character has to pay to ensure audience sympathy is that he must renounce his previous role as the spokesman of those who reject assimilation. Not until Walter Hill's *Geronimo: An American Legend* (1993) does Geronimo's story get told with anything like a fair representation of the case for Indian separateness.

In *Broken Arrow* only one alternative to that embraced by Geronimo is presented to Cochise, that of embracing the white way of life, and he accepts it. But in posing such a stark dilemma the film shows how locked in it is to the thinking of the 1950s. Despite its liberal pretensions, it has no conception of the actual history of Indian peoples up to the mid-twentieth century. Either Apache culture is preserved as it always was, which is impossible, or it is obliterated, the Apache nomads and raiders turned into settled farmers indistinguishable from the Americans. Assimilation is their inevitable fate. Yet far from being either assimilated or withering away, Indian numbers were increasing in the 1950s and Indian cultures gathering strength. True, Indians lived under terrible disadvantages, and still do. In all the indicators of physical and moral health, such as infant mortality or alcoholism or educational attainment, Indians lag behind all other groups. But despite this, Indians have not gone away, nor have they become whites.

The policy of 'termination' proved not to be the last twist in the ever-evolving history of relations between Indians and the US government. During the 1970s the concept of tribal sovereignty replaced termination as official policy. Increasingly Indians were awarded a separate legal status. Tribes were encouraged to register with the government and thereby assume responsibility for public funds granted for social services. Once such registration was achieved, the tribes themselves could decide who might be admitted to membership. The legal status of reservations also allowed them to bypass laws against gambling and establish profitable casinos, and to avoid certain taxes. An act of Congress in 1978 guaranteed Indian religious freedom, including the sacred use of the drug peyote. Thus in a number of ways Indians were taking back the sovereignty that they had originally been granted by the treaties of earlier times.

Broken Arrow cannot foresee such developments, cannot envisage a third way, neither assimilation nor obliteration, in which Indians are separate but equal, with a viable culture and way of life that is different from whites, a culture that does not remain the same (for what culture does?) but which develops under its own historical momentum while still retaining its roots. In 1950 this was inconceivable even to liberals.

Broken Arrow is not the first post-war Western to take a sympathetic view of Indians. The opening film of John Ford's 'cavalry trilogy', *Fort Apache* (1948), features none other than Cochise, who is presented as a dignified and honourable man. The massacre of the cavalry that concludes the film is brought about not by Indian aggression but by the arrogance and obstinacy of their commander, Colonel Thursday (Henry Fonda). In the second film of the trilogy, *She Wore a Yellow Ribbon* (1949), after the defeat of Custer in 1876 the Indians of the plains are on the warpath. Fortunately Captain Brittles (John Wayne) is a friend of the wise old chief Pony That Walks (played by Chief Big Tree), and together they conceive a ruse to deflect the young braves away from war.

Ford's attitude to Indians merits an essay in itself, veering as it does all the way from the apologia of *Cheyenne*

John Wayne with Chief Big Tree in John Ford's *She Wore a Yellow Ribbon* (1949).

Autumn (1964) to the crude racism of an early episode in *My Darling Clementine* (1946), in which Wyatt Earp (Henry Fonda) arrests a drunken Indian who is shooting up the town. Having knocked him on the head, Earp kicks him ignominiously up the backside: 'Indian, get out of town and stay out.' The Indian is played by Charlie Stevens, who had a lengthy career in movies and was Geronimo's grandson, no less.

However, the success of *Broken Arrow* undoubtedly paved the way for a wave of Indian films in the 1950s. What is striking, on viewing a representative sample, is the extent to which the films attempt, within the limits of generic constraints, to take a positive view. There are more than fifty Westerns in the decade that deal in some substantial way with Indians. I've been able to view about forty of these and there are some clear patterns. In the first place, hardly any of them adopt what could be called a overtly racist or hostile attitude to Indians per se. Among the exceptions is *Dakota Incident* (1956), in which Ward Bond plays a US Senator out west caught up in an Indian attack on a stagecoach. He's an ignorant blowhard who is ridiculed on account of the liberal claptrap he spouts about his Indian 'brothers'. The film takes evident satisfaction in a scene where the Senator tries to reason with the Indians and preach peace, and is shot full of arrows for his pains. Even so, although the film has spent ninety minutes dismissing any talk of peace, one character feels obliged to confess at the end, rather unconvincingly, that the Senator 'tried to sow the seeds' of reconciliation. The most nakedly hostile film I've seen from this period is *Arrowhead* (1953), in which Charlton Heston plays Ed Bannon, a scout who has lived with the Apache and knows their ways but is implacably antagonistic and mistrustful towards them. The Apache leader Toriano (Jack Palance) is a fitting match, equally determined to kill all the whites he can. In a hand-to-hand combat at the end, Bannon breaks Toriano's neck.

Far more typical than such expressions of enmity are the many films in which violence between whites and Indians is caused by white racists, who often have ulterior motives for their acts. Sometimes, as in *The Half-Breed* (1952), *Sitting Bull* (1954), *Drums Across the River* (1954), *Chief Crazy Horse* (1955) and *The Indian Fighter* (1955), there is gold on the Indian reservation and unscrupulous whites hatch schemes to get at it, thus provoking the Indians into violence in order to defend their lands. In *The Great Sioux Uprising* (1953) crooked horse-trader Lyle Bettger wants to steal the Indians' horses and sell them to the Union army. Naturally, Red Cloud (John War Eagle) objects. Sometimes it is the Indians' land itself that the whites covet for their farms and livestock, as in *Devil's Doorway* (1950) and *Seminole* (1953). Scott Simmon has observed that such characters are also present in early silent Westerns, and refers to them as 'scapegoats', conveniently diverting attention away from the actual historical forces that brought about the dispossession of the Indians, for which we might all feel some responsibility.[8] However, it's worth remembering that the privileging of individual motive above social forces as a cause for action is a feature of Hollywood cinema generally, not merely of the Western. Early in its formation Hollywood discovered that the personal had more appeal than the political.

Sometimes white hostility is pathological: in *The Last Hunt* (1956) Robert Taylor shoots Indians for fun. In several films white society proves intolerant of mixed-race marriages. In *Broken Lance* (1954) the governor of the state refuses to let his daughter marry Joe (Robert Wagner), the son of Matt Devereaux (Spencer Tracy) by his Indian wife (Katy Jurado). There is similar prejudice in two films from 1960, *Flaming Star* and *The Unforgiven*. In the former, Elvis Presley is Pacer, the son of a white father and a Kiowa woman (Dolores del Rio), torn between his two heritages when hostilities break out. Admittedly his mother's people are against her marriage too, but it is from the whites that the most vicious enmity comes. In *The Unforgiven* Audrey Hepburn is also a Kiowa, adopted by a white family. When hostilities develop between

Katy Jurado in Edward
Dmytryk's *Broken Lance*
(1954).

Dolores del Rio and Elvis
Presley in Don Siegel's
Flaming Star (1960).

the whites and the Indians, she is called a 'dirty Indian' by a neighbour, and her own stepbrother (Audie Murphy) turns against her.

Another cause of trouble with the Indians is the army. In *They Rode West* (1954) Phil Carey is an army officer who attempts to prevent the fort doctor (Robert Francis) from treating the neighbouring Kiowa, who are suffering from malaria. This provokes an Indian attack on the fort. In *Tomahawk* (1951) Alex Nichol is a vicious Indian hater, an army man who has participated in the notorious Chivington Massacre of the Cheyenne at Sand Creek in 1864. He does his best to provoke a war with Red Cloud's Sioux. Following Colonel Thursday in *Fort Apache*, a parade of martinets in blue uniforms marches through the Western of the 1950s, variously portrayed by Jeff Chandler in *Two Flags West* (1950), Robert Preston in *The Last Frontier* (1955), Ainslie Prior (as the egregious Colonel Chivington) in *The Guns of Fort Petticoat* (1957), Rhodes Reason in *Yellowstone Kelly* (1959) and Richard Carlson in *Seminole*. The obstinacy, ignorance of Indian ways and lack of sympathy for their plight displayed by these incompetent commanders invariably provoke unnecessary conflict.

Indians are given frequent opportunities in these films to protest against white behaviour and to state their case. In *The Great Sioux Uprising* Red Cloud (John War Eagle) accuses the whites of speaking 'with twin tongues' because of the treaties they have broken. In *Tomahawk* Red Cloud (again played by John War Eagle) shows himself to be a reasonable man. He laments that as a result of white intrusion the sacred hunting grounds are 'silent and empty' and that there is 'starvation and sickness where once there was plenty'. He says that he would make his people learn the ways of the white man if only he was given time, but that the whites are pushing too hard. In *Chief Crazy Horse* the Sioux are promised at the Treaty of Laramie that the Black Hills will remain theirs for ever; Victor Mature as Crazy Horse is understandably incensed when this promise is broken. In *War Paint* (1953) the Indian Taslik (Keith Larsen) is suspicious of the treaty he is being offered, based on past experience: 'When we cry for food you will tell us to eat grass.' His sister Wanima (Joan Taylor) is equally reluctant to agree to anything that will undermine Indian independence: 'Soon the other whites will come and spit on the people when we are weak.' In *Flaming Star* Buffalo Horn (Rudolfo Acosta) tries to persuade the half-Indian Pacer to side with the Kiowa. Whose land is this, he demands? It's the whites who cause the trouble: 'Forever taking, forever pushing.' Sometimes the whites put the case for the Indians. In *The Big Sky* (1952) trapper Arthur Hunnicutt contrasts Indian generosity with white acquisitiveness: 'White men don't see nothing pretty but that they want to grab it.'

Of course not all Indians are deserving of sympathy. Just as in *Broken Arrow*, there is frequently a divide between the good Indians (those who are willing to compromise and even adopt the ways of the whites) and those who are implacably opposed to white expansion, choosing to fight to the death. In *Drum Beat* (1954) Charles Bronson plays Captain Jack, the leader of the Modoc Indians during their war against

Alan Ladd (seated) with Charles Bronson as Captain Jack in Delmer Daves's *Drum Beat* (1954).

the whites of 1872–3. He is hostile, headstrong and eager for war. At the end of the film he is hanged. By contrast, a beautiful young Modoc girl, Toby (Marisa Pavan), and her brother Manok (Anthony Caruso) earnestly desire peace. In *Seminole*, chief Osceola is played by Anthony Quinn. Presented (in accordance with historical fact) as half-white, he tries to achieve peace with the whites through negotiations with his childhood friend, an army officer played by Rock Hudson. But just as the counter-balance to Hudson is the pig-headed Major Degan ('my orders are to flush them out and drive them west'), so on the Seminole side Kajeck (Hugh O'Brian) demands that the Seminole go to war. In *Across the Wide Missouri* (1950) the elderly Bear Ghost (Jack Holt) is friendly towards the visiting white trappers, but the younger Ironshirt (Ricardo Montalban) wants to fight them. Similarly, in *Sitting Bull* the eponymous Sioux chief (J. Carroll Naish) tries to keep his people in check when whites make incursions onto Indian land, but Crazy Horse (Iron Eyes Cody) wants to fight. Those who counsel war are almost invariably defeated, and often killed. Though the films often lean over backwards to show that the Indians are provoked into warfare, those who favour violence rather than negotiation are seen as at best romantics who refuse to face the inevitable, or, as in *Broken Arrow*, obstinate and recalcitrant enemies of peace whose path must lead to disaster.

The most striking thing about the Indian Westerns of this period is their almost obsessive interest in the question of mixed marriage. The way these relationships are dealt with suggests that they dramatize white sexual anxieties rather than acting as models for the eventual assimilation of the Indians. Fully half of the forty films viewed contain a character who engages in some sort of sexual relationship across the racial divide, but never without difficulty; that is to say, the relationships are never 'normal' or 'natural' – instead there is always a problem of some kind. As Angela Aleiss notes, the Production Code, a voluntary code of practice instituted by the major studios in the 1930s, forbade the representation of sexual relations between white and black, but made no mention of sex between whites and Indians. However, the films are fully aware that there is a social taboo against such alliances, one that invariably arouses comment within the film, as well as supplying the relationship with an exotically erotic charge.

In most cases it is an Indian woman who takes up with a white man: white patriarchal desire has the power to overcome prejudice. Such a relationship is central to *Across the Wide Missouri*, *The Last Hunt*, *The Big Sky*, *The Indian Fighter*, *Broken Lance* and several others. Invariably the Indian 'maiden' is beautiful, often the daughter of a chief. In several films, such as *The Indian Fighter* and *The Last Hunt*, as well as in *Duel in the Sun*, dating from 1946, she is seen swimming naked, testament to the free and easy sensuality attributed to women of other races. Sometimes, as in *Across the Wide Missouri*, the relationship is doomed, as it is in *Broken Arrow*. In *Tomahawk* and *Distant Drums* (1951), the Indian wife of the hero has already been killed before the film begins. It is as if the filmmakers, taken aback at their audacity in depicting such a

Elsa Martinelli and Kirk Douglas go swimming in André de Toth's *The Indian Fighter* (1955).

transgressive union, need to introduce the woman's death in order to mitigate the offence: the only good Indian wife is a dead Indian wife. However, there are several happy endings: in *Yellowstone Kelly*, in which Clint Walker is the hero who, when initially asked his opinion about intermarriage replies, 'It just won't work', but who finally commits himself to the beautiful Arapaho girl Wahleeah (Andra Martin); in *The Indian Fighter*, in the last scene of which Kirk Douglas goes swimming with his Sioux girlfriend Elsa Martinelli; in *The Last Hunt*, in which Stewart Granger rides away with Debra Paget; in *Run of the Arrow* (1957), in which former Confederate soldier Rod Steiger remains with his Sioux wife at the end of the film, and in *White Feather* (1955), in which Robert Wagner is left happily gazing into the eyes of Appearing Day, a Cheyenne girl acted, once more, by Debra Paget, who, after her success as Sonseeahray in *Broken Arrow* made something of a career out of playing beautiful Indian maidens, before playing an Indian of another kind in Fritz Lang's pair of oriental romances *The Tiger of Eschnapur* (1959) and *The Indian Tomb* (1959).

Hollywood clearly found the notion of an Indian man having sexual relations with a white woman altogether more difficult. We have already seen the fate of the Navajo Indian who loves a white woman in *The Vanishing American* (1925). In *Devil's Doorway* (1950) Robert Taylor is a Shoshone who seems to be falling for a white female lawyer (Paula Raymond), but draws back ('In a hundred years from now it might have worked') before he is killed in a final confrontation with the cavalry. Similarly, in *Seminole* the half-Indian Osceola, who

Robert Taylor and James Mitchell in Anthony Mann's *Devil's Doorway* (1950).

loves a white woman, is killed before the end of the film, allowing her to marry army officer Rock Hudson. In *Brave Warrior* (1952), the Shawnee chief Tecumseh (played by genuine Indian Jay Silverheels) loves Laura (Christine Larsen), the daughter of a white trader. But after the disaster of the battle of Tippecanoe (1811) he gives up his claim to her and renounces any attempt to integrate with white society.

Several of the films that present relations between white women and Indian men do so through the structure of the captivity narrative. Well known is John Ford's *The Searchers* (1956), in which Ethan (John Wayne) rescues his niece Debbie (Natalie Wood), but only after she has become the wife of Comanche chief Scar (Henry Brandon), a relationship that revolts Ethan, an avowed racist, but is viewed more tolerantly by others. At the end of the film Ethan scalps Scar, an act which it is difficult not to interpret as a symbolic castration. Less known is *Trooper Hook* (1957), in which Barbara Stanwyck plays Cora, a white woman who has been captured by the Apache Nanchez (Rudolfo Acosta) and has had a son by him. Whereas Debbie is welcomed back by her family, Cora finds only white racism and is rejected by her white husband, although she eventually finds consolation in the arms of army sergeant Hook (Joel McCrea). In *The Charge at Feather River* (1953) Guy Madison leads an expedition to rescue two white captives from the Cheyenne. One of them, Ann (Helen Westcott), is fearful; the implication is that she has been raped, and she dreads the scrutiny of the 'prim and proper' white women when she is returned to civilization. The younger girl, Jenny (Vera Miles), has become acculturated, being betrothed to Thunderhawk, the Cheyenne chief (Fred Carson); she defends the character of her Indian captors and looks forward to being rescued back again by them. In view of what is seen as her excessive enthusiasm for the Indian way of life, it is not surprising that while attempting to escape she falls to her death. The implication is that white people should show sympathy for the woman taken against her will, but not for one who rushes into an Indian's arms.

Such a view of captivity, however, is not shared by all the films of this period. In *They Rode West* Robert Francis discovers that a Kiowa woman, Manyi-ten (May Wynn), is in fact a white captive, married to the brother of chief Satanta. When her husband dies Francis tries to persuade her to return to white society, but she has no desire to do so. In Ford's *Two Rode Together*, made in 1962 and only just outside the period of our sample, James Stewart rescues a white woman captive (Linda Cristal) from the Comanche. She has been the wife of Stone Calf (Woody Strode). When questioned about her life she admits conditions were harsh, but she grieves for her husband when Stewart kills him, and once back at the fort she experiences such unpleasant treatment by other white women that she wishes she had never been rescued.

Despite these exceptions, it is clear that in Hollywood's eyes the policy of assimilation became problematic when extended into the sexual domain. Social attitudes of the 1950s assumed that the wife took the subordinate position, symbolized by the adoption of the husband's name. Thus when white men take Indian wives, even though there were difficulties, the Indian qualities of the wife would become secondary to her 'white' identity. But when Indian men wished to take white women, it appeared that assimilation only worked one way. Whites, whether male or female, are not to be assimilated into Indian society.

Undoubtedly, the Indian Westerns of the 1950s are limited in their perspective. Indians are seen through white eyes, 'good' if they are reasonable and will listen to white arguments, 'bad' if they continue to resist. In *They Rode West* army doctor Robert Francis tells the Kiowa that ultimately it

O'Meara (Rod Steiger, centre) in the camp of the Sioux in Sam Fuller's *Run of the Arrow* (1957), with Blue Buffalo (Charles Bronson), Yellow Moccasin (Sarita Montiel) and Crazy Wolf (H. M. Wynant).

is useless to kill whites. More will always come to replace them. This is an argument frequently heard: history is on the side of the whites, and in the end that is what matters. Even so, there is something impressive about the constant pleas for tolerance that run through these films, the willingness to identify white racism and recognize Indian grievances, and even, on occasion, to manifest curiosity about another culture. The heroes are frequently those who know Indians, have lived among them, like Yellowstone Kelly and like the Stewart

Granger character in *The Last Hunt*. Admittedly this curiosity usually goes only so far, although in *Run of the Arrow* Rod Steiger, who has come to live among the Sioux, engages in a discussion of comparative religion with Blue Buffalo (Charles Bronson). Mostly the heroes have acquired scraps of useful information rather than any deep understanding of another culture, such as how to recognize the different styles of Cheyenne and Comanche arrows, or why it is that Indians won't fight at night, a topic that crops up with surprising frequency. Even so, with rare exceptions, such as Ethan in *The Searchers* and Bannon in *Arrowhead*, familiarity with Indian ways brings not contempt but sympathy and even admiration.

By 1971 views of Indians were changing, moving beyond the limited alternatives offered in *Broken Arrow*. A major anthropological work declared:

> Arguments about the future of the first Americans have commonly focused on two alternatives: should Indian culture and identity be 'preserved' and ways found for Indians to support themselves 'as Indians,' or should Indians be helped to 'assimilate' and become absorbed into the 'mainstream of American life'? One thesis of this book is that these are not the only alternatives; that Indians have played a role in American history, and that they still have a role to play, neither as 'museum pieces' nor as individuals lost in 'the melting pot,' but as Indians of the twentieth century. Indian

traditions have neither fossilized nor disappeared; Indian ways of today are not those of centuries ago but they are nonetheless Indian. Indian cultural traditions have continued to grow and change, and there has been constant integration of innovations into characteristically Indian ways and Indian views. Today there is a strong interest in defining these ways.[9]

Indian Westerns too were changing. True, Hollywood showed as little interest as it ever did in contemporary Indians. But its view of the past was developing. *Cheyenne Autumn* (1964) was John Ford's attempt to set the record straight about the ways in which the US government had maltreated the Indians. A sincere if occasionally ponderous film, it tried hard to give the Cheyenne dignity, even if all the major Indian roles were played by non-Indian actors. At the end of the decade, *Tell Them Willie Boy Is Here* (1969), based on a historical incident, recounted the pursuit of a Paiute Indian at the turn of the century, chased into the desert and eventually killed by a racist white posse. Its director, the formerly blacklisted Abraham Polonsky, explicitly connected his film to the Vietnam war, which was increasingly dominating American politics.

Parallels with Vietnam were intended in two films made the following year. The first, *Soldier Blue*, dramatizes the Sand Creek Massacre of the Cheyenne from 1864, in which a volunteer force under Colonel Chivington attacked a peaceful village, killing more than two hundred Indians and sexually mutilating the bodies. At the time the film appeared, the infamous My Lai massacre of a Vietnamese village by American forces had recently come to light. This contemporary atrocity is also evoked in *Little Big Man* (1970), which enacts the attack by the Seventh Cavalry under George Armstrong Custer upon a Cheyenne village on the Washita, in Oklahoma in 1868, in which women and children were killed indiscriminately.

Two other films from this period attempted more detailed pictures of Indian life than Hollywood had previously achieved. *A Man Called Horse* (1970) is about an English nobleman (Richard Harris) who is captured by the Sioux and gradually assimilates to their culture. The film's director, Elliot Silverstein, went to some trouble to ensure ethnographic accuracy and hired Clyde Dollar, a historian of the Sioux, to ensure accuracy. However, the fact that Dollar was a white man aroused the hostility of Russell Means, a Sioux actor and activist, and many Indians criticized the film's representation of Indian culture, not assisted perhaps by the casting of Corinna Tsopei, a Greek and a former Miss Universe, as Running Deer, the Sioux woman the hero takes as a wife.[10]

In *Jeremiah Johnson* (1972) Robert Redford plays a mountain man in the 1840s who takes an Indian wife (later killed) and through no fault of his own gets involved in a feud with the Crow Indians. Despite this enmity, Johnson has great respect for the Indians and for the environment, unlike most of the white men in the film. But in the same year a very different film tested the limits of the rather too easily achieved liberalism that had become the norm in Hollywood's treatment of Indians. *Ulzana's Raid* (1972), directed by Robert Aldrich, poses radical questions about the policy of assimilation, intended to bridge the differences between whites and Indians. It shows the Apaches as capable of horrifying violence: white men are tortured and their bodies mutilated, white women are raped. The explicit nature of the violence shown appears to be a deliberate refusal to 'sentimentalize' Indian behaviour in the manner of such pro-Indian films of the early 1970s as *Little Big Man* (1970), in which the Cheyenne function as surrogate hippies, tolerant of homosexuality, kind to children, engaging in free love and conversations about the meaning of life. A

Jorge Luke as Ke-Ni-Tay in Robert Aldrich's *Ulzana's Raid* (1972).

similar pro-Indian view emerges in *Billy Jack* (1971), Tom Laughlin's film about contemporary reservation life, in which the hero fights a one-man battle for Indian rights. Made outside the studio system, the film caught the mood of the anti-war generation and the protest movement, and its success allowed Laughlin to make two sequels.

By contrast, in *Ulzana's Raid* the audience have their faces rubbed in some brutal facts about the wars against the Apache. The young lieutenant leading the soldiers in pursuit of the murderous Ulzana is the son of a Christian minister, and seeks to understand what makes the Indians so merciless. He interrogates Ke-Ni-Tay, the Apache scout who is working for the army:

> 'Why are your people like that? Why are they so cruel? . . . '
> 'Is how they are.'
> 'But why?'
> 'Is how they are, they have always been that way.'

The scout explains that Ulzana has felt his power ebb away through being confined on the reservation. Killing white men will bring it back. Such behaviour is incomprehensible to the lieutenant, but the film suggests that the Apache are different; they always have been and, the implication is clear, always will be. The film does not preach a policy of separate but equal, but it acknowledges that there is an irreducible difference, and it is careful to show at the same time that

Wes Studi as the evil Magua in Michael Mann's *The Last of the Mohicans* (1992).

whites are also capable of vindictive violence when some soldiers mutilate the body of a dead Apache, an act which, as the veteran scout MacIntosh (Burt Lancaster), who has an Indian wife, remarks wryly, 'kind of confuses the issue, don't it?'

The Western went into a decline in the 1970s as Holly-wood lost interest in a genre that appeared played out. In the 1990s there were brief signs of a revival with Michael Mann's remake of *The Last of the Mohicans* (1992), which rewrote Cooper's novel so as to allow a romance between the hero, Natty Bumppo (Daniel Day-Lewis), and Cora (Madeleine Stowe), one of the colonel's daughters he rescues from the evil Indian Magua (Wes Studi). The parallel but interracial romance between his Indian friend Uncas (Eric Schweig) and Alice (Jodhi May), the other daughter, is relegated to a minor place in the film; once again, it does not survive the end of the film, since Alice jumps to her death to escape the clutches of Magua.

The most successful of the Westerns of the decade was *Dances With Wolves* (1990). Kevin Costner's films are not

Bad Indians: The Pawnees on the attack in Kevin Costner's *Dances With Wolves* (1990).

universally popular and he seems to have the knack of rubbing some people up the wrong way, but he has done more than anyone since Clint Eastwood to keep the Western going as a viable movie genre, directing *Dances With Wolves* (1990) and *Open Range* (2003), both of which he starred in, and appearing in *Silverado* (1985) and *Wyatt Earp* (1994). *Dances With Wolves* was astonishingly successful, winning Oscars for Best Picture and Best Director, and making a good deal of money. Yet almost from the start it ran into controversy. Despite Costner's evident good intentions and his desire to make a film that was in every way positive about Indians, opposition came from a number of quarters.

The story is simple enough. Sent west at his own request after a near-suicidal charge on a Civil War battlefield is interpreted as heroism, Union soldier John Dunbar finds himself posted to a fort on the prairie where he is the sole occupant. Gradually he makes friends with a group of Sioux

Indians, is adopted into the tribe and marries a white woman captive. Arrested by the army and charged with treasonable desertion, he is rescued by his Indian friends, but eventually sets out on his own, fearful that his presence will bring down the army's wrath upon the Sioux.

Costner's film is notable in at least two respects. Firstly, all the speaking parts for Indians (and there are many, some of them almost as large as Costner's own) had Indian actors cast in the role. Graham Greene, who plays the Sioux holy man Kicking Bird, has one of the largest parts ever given to a Native American actor. Secondly, when the Indians speak, they use native languages and their words are translated into English by subtitles. No more of the 'How! Me heap big chief.' However, although all the actors playing Sioux are Native Americans, very few spoke Lakota, the language of the Sioux. Doris Leader Charge, who also plays the role of Pretty Shield in the film, had to be employed to translate the script into Lakota and to coach the actors in speaking the language.

Kevin Costner and Graham Greene in *Dances With Wolves*.

Dances With Wolves probably went further than any previous Hollywood film towards presenting a positive and fully rounded view of Indians. Dunbar is full of praise for the Sioux, writing in his journal: 'I've never known a people so eager to laugh, so devoted to family, so dedicated to each other, and the only word that comes to mind is "harmony".' By contrast, the whites we encounter are brutish, dirty and do nothing but desecrate the land. The fort to which Dunbar finds himself posted is a garbage dump, with its water polluted by dead animals, and later Dunbar and Kicking Bird find the camp of white hunters, where again decomposing dead animals are piled high. When slaughtering the buffalo, the whites take only a tiny part of the animal, leaving the rest to rot. The view that Indians are the true ecologists is given full support in this film.

Despite this, the film aroused considerable opposition. In at least two respects it seemed to fall short of being the wholly positive contribution towards the representation of Indian life that it seemed to aspire to. Dunbar is so enamoured of the Sioux that he wishes to become one, to merge his white identity into an Indian one (after he acquires an Indian name he says, 'When I heard my Sioux name being called over and over I knew for the first time who I really was.'). But the Sioux are not the only Indians in the film. Midway through they are set upon by a band of marauding Pawnees, whose physical appearance is fearsome, their faces painted black, their hair partly shaved. The Pawnees attack the Sioux village when most of the men are absent, leaving only women, children and the aged. Dunbar has no hesitation in seeing them as enemies and leads the Sioux resistance. It seems that the concept of good and bad Indians, which in fiction goes back as far as Fenimore Cooper and beyond, is still alive. Good Indians are those that whites can identify with. Bad Indians are those who threaten this process. (Interestingly, in Michael Blake's original novel the Indians who befriend Dunbar are not Sioux, but Comanche – traditionally, in the cinema, a people implacably hostile to whites, as in John Ford's *The Searchers*.)

This being a Hollywood film, it is almost inevitable that there should be a romance. Dunbar is presented as a man without a history: therefore he is in need of a wife. Given the decision to go for realism in the presentation of Indian language, the plot device of having a white woman captive available to act as interpreter is a necessary one. But there is no inevitable reason why Dunbar should choose her as his companion. The suspicion arises that those who shaped the script avoided the more complete integration of Dunbar into the Sioux nation that would have come about had he taken an Indian wife. Miscegenation, it seems, is still a step too far for Hollywood.

These defects do not fatally damage the film's claims to be a sympathetic portrait. Still less do the charges of some hostile critics that details of the costumes or customs of the Indians are inauthentic, such as, for example, that the Indians' horses, contrary to practice, appear to be shod. The filmmakers seemingly went to some trouble to get things right, and pedantic observations on possible inaccuracies do not substantially detract from the film's merits. However, there were further charges against the film that are more fundamental and go to the heart of its status as an exemplary work. In her book *Going Native*, Shari M. Huhndorf contends that however positive the image, the Indians in the film exist primarily as the means whereby Dunbar achieves redemption from the despair that has possessed him at the beginning of the film. It's not a film primarily about Indians, but about a white man's spiritual journey. And its overarching ideological project, the goal it seeks to achieve in the wider context of history, is to show that there is at least one good white man, who cares and understands, and thus can absolve us collectively from our guilt:

> By going native, Dunbar sheds the culpability associated with his official army duties as an 'Indian fighter'. Significantly, because his perspective provides the film's narrative center and thus the white audiences' point of identification, it also symbolically purges white America of its responsibility for the terrible plights of Native Americans, past and present.[11]

The question of guilt is perhaps not quite such a simple one as Huhndorf supposes. In what sense am I, born in the middle of the twentieth century, responsible for something that happened in a previous century? It's a bit like making each succeeding generation of Germans take responsibility for the crimes of the Nazis. Speaking less moralistically and more practically, how far is it realistic to demand of a multi-million dollar epic, made with the intention of securing a profit, that it renounce the device, proven effective during a century of filmmaking, of offering a point of identification that the majority of the potential audience will find appealing? Indians, as we have seen, make up only 1.5 per cent of the potential audience inside the USA.

There's no doubt that telling the story through the eyes of a white man skews the film's view of Indians. For Dunbar, the Sioux are the exact opposite of the white society he has rejected; what he finds is what he has been looking for. Yet the question of identification is more complex than Huhndorf's argument allows. Near the end of the film, Dunbar has been captured by the army and is being carried away to court martial and probable execution. His captors are brutal and vindictive, but none the less they are white. Earlier, Dunbar has witnessed the aftermath of the Sioux's attack on the white buffalo hunters. He sees hanging up in the Indian camp a white man's hand and a white scalp. He is repelled, and confesses: 'The gap between us was greater than I ever could have imagined.' Yet by the end of the film, when the Sioux come to rescue him from his captors, the white audience is by this time undoubtedly identifying with the Sioux, to the extent that they surely cheer on the Sioux in their assault on the white soldiers. When the young Sioux boy Smiles A Lot kills a white sergeant, we feel that justice has been done. The white audience now identifies with the Indians.

Shari Huhndorf makes a related point about the ending of the film. An elegiac caption laments the passing of the 'great horse culture of the plains'. The Indians are only seen living in the past; their way of life has been destroyed by the white society that has succeeded them. There's an important issue here. By being set in a historical era long gone, Westerns about Indians almost inevitably have a nostalgic tinge. However liberal in their intentions, they celebrate what is assumed to be over. What they don't ever do is present the living Indians of today. Huhndorf asserts that in consequence they reinforce the claims of white European–Americans as the 'proper heirs' of the land.[12] The question is whether nostalgia for a vanished way of life is necessarily a denial of the present. Must any historical film inevitably be a strategy to shut out present-day realities? It is certainly true that Hollywood has almost wholly avoided making films about present-day Indian life. Whether this is because it has preferred to use the Western as a vehicle for justifying what was done to the Indians in the name of civilization and progress, or whether the Indian audience is not large enough to sustain films about itself, or whether the subject would inevitably be too grim for an industry dedicated to 'entertainment', Hollywood has steered well clear of the reservation as a subject for drama.

There seems only one way that this is likely to change. In Thomas King's novel *Green Grass, Running Water* an Indian child watches television:

> 'Mom, is this the one where the cavalry comes over the hill and kills the Indians?'
> 'Probably.'

'How come the Indians always get killed?'

'It's just a movie.'

'But what if they won?'

'Well,' Latisha said, watching her son rub his dirty socks up and down the wall, 'if the Indians won, it probably wouldn't be a Western.'[13]

This suggests that the Western has a built-in ideology, one in which the defeat of the Indian is inevitable. And in a sense this is true, since the films are based, however loosely, on history and the Indians did not 'win'. History is irreversible, although the lesson drawn from Indian defeat can be changed, from a celebration of white triumph to an acknowledgement of the human cost. But if we want films that look not to the past but to the present and future of Indians, then we shall probably have to look to Indian filmmakers to produce them.

As it turned out, *Dances With Wolves* did prove to have a connection to contemporary Indian life, but in a way its creators did not foresee. Kevin Costner decided to invest some of the vast profits that the film had made in the construction of an entertainment complex in the Black Hills of South Dakota. This area is considered by many Sioux as a sacred place, and indeed as the spot from which the Sioux first emerged onto the earth. Anthropologists maintain that the Sioux did not migrate west from Minnesota until the 1770s, but nevertheless in 1980 the Supreme Court acknowledged that the Black Hills had been unfairly taken from the Sioux under treaties made in the nineteenth century, and awarded the tribe more than $100 million in compensation. Surprisingly to some, the Sioux have refused the money, and have sued for the return of the land. The Black Hills have now become a *cause célèbre* of Indian nationalism.

Despite the prior existence of numerous tourist facilities in the region, many of them tacky and tasteless, Costner's proposal to build his resort there soon became a focus for Indian radicalism. He was accused of betraying the very people he had made his money from, the Sioux. To date, though Costner and his brother Daniel have built a casino, the Midnight Star, in Deadwood, they have yet to develop the 600-acre site they acquired on the edge of town, where they planned a hotel and golf course. What this affair proves, if nothing else, is that making Westerns about 'the Indian problem' is a lot more of a political issue than it used to be.[14]

Indians have a long tradition of making art of one kind or another, though the primary significance of most of the objects produced before contact with whites seems to have been religious rather than aesthetic. Indians have excelled in the decorative arts and crafts such as pottery, textiles and jewellery. Representational painting also has a lengthy history, with rock paintings in the south-west dating back to the Anasazi period, centuries before the arrival of the Spanish. In the second half of the nineteenth century Indians in reservations or in government captivity began to portray their lives in the form of so-called 'ledger' paintings, named for the accounting ledger books from which the paper was usually taken. These pictures, not following European-derived rules of scale and perspective, have great freshness and immediacy. In the twentieth century various schools of Indian painting emerged, including the 'Kiowa Five', a group of painters trained at the University of Oklahoma in the 1920s, the Santa Fe Movement of the 1930s, and later the work emanating from the Institute of American Indian Arts in the 1960s. More recently, Jimmie Durham, a Cherokee artist and activist, has produced paintings and sculptures that offer a wry commentary on white perceptions of Indians, as for example in his creation *Pocahontas' Underwear* (1985), a pair of women's knickers made of red feathers and beads, which both plays upon the eroticization of the female Indian and is also a joke at the expense of po-faced white anthropologists.[15]

Photography too has become an important means for Indians to represent themselves. Indian photographers such as Hulleah Tsinhnahjinnie have produced pictures that work against the stereotypes of Indian representation.[16] In literature, novelists such as Leslie Marmon Silko and N. Scott Momaday have produced classics of Indian fiction. Louise Erdrich, Thomas King and Louis Owens are among more recent novelists to have made their mark, creating a body of work that is definably Indian in its sensibility. In their fictions, Indians represent themselves, for themselves; it is not the primary intention to represent Indians to whites.

Given the greater material resources required, it is not surprising that filmmaking has proved a more difficult undertaking. *Wiping the War Paint off the Lens*, a survey of films about Indians made by Indians, estimates that there are more than a thousand titles in existence.[17] But almost all of them are documentaries, often produced for public television; new works are screened every two years at a Native American Film and Video Festival. Feature films made by Indians require much greater resources and have only just begun to emerge. For several years the prestigious Sundance Festival has been running a Native American Initiative, which programmes Native films at its annual festival in Utah, invites aspirant Native filmmakers to its Producers' Conference to network with other independent filmmakers, and offers assistance and advice to between two and four projects a year.

One beneficiary of this programme is Sherman Alexie, a Spokane/Coeur d'Alene Indian whose wry and witty stories and novels have given him a high literary profile. One of the short stories from his first published collection, *The Lone Ranger and Tonto Fistfight in Heaven*,[18] formed the basis of a screenplay for the feature film *Smoke Signals* (1999), which was directed by Chris Eyre (Cheyenne/Arapaho). Credited as the first American feature film with Native American actors, writer and director, the film was picked up for distribution by Miramax after winning awards at the 1998 Sundance Festival and achieved both critical and box-office success.

It's the story of Victor and Thomas, two friends from the Coeur d'Alene reservation. Victor has been deserted by his father at an early age. When his father's death is reported in Phoenix, Arizona, the two set off to retrieve his ashes. The film deals with problems of reservation life such as alcoholism and

Evan Adams as Thomas, with his 'fry-bread power' sweater, in Chris Eyre's *Smoke Signals* (1998).

unemployment, but is full of Alexei's quirky humour and acute observations of Indian experience. In the Greyhound bus on the way down to Arizona, Victor lectures Thomas on how to be a real Indian. He needs to 'get stoic' and look 'like a warrior'. The ever-willing Thomas buys a t-shirt with the slogan 'Frybread Power', but observes when two rednecks usurp their seats on the bus that the warrior style doesn't seem to get results. Later Thomas comments scornfully that 'the only one thing more pathetic than Indians on TV is Indians watching Indians on TV.' Victor, hostile to his father's memory because of his drinking and violence, finally achieves some sort of reconciliation through the intervention of a young Indian woman, Suzie, who had befriended his father after he had deserted Victor.

Though there are some interactions with whites, it's not fundamentally a film about white-Indian relations but about Indians together, specific enough to give a glimpse for non-Indian audiences into reservation life but general enough to have a universal appeal. Subsequently Alexie has ventured into direction, with *The Business of Fancydancing* (2002), made with several of the same actors (Evan Adams, Michelle St John) who appeared in *Smoke Signals*. These are the first shoots of what may prove to be a significant incursion into theatrical feature production by Indians. Elsewhere in North America there have been other important developments. *Atanarjuat: The Fast Runner* (2000) is a film made in the Inuktitut language of the native peoples of the Canadian Arctic. Set in the distant past, long before whites arrived, the film cast native actors and is directed by Zacharias Kunuk, the first of his family to read, write and make films.

These modest beginnings show that an Indian cinema is possible. Digital technology will make independent film-making cheaper, even if access to distribution networks will still be difficult. But Indian films will never challenge Hollywood on its home ground. We won't get alternative Westerns, in which the Indians win, because if Indians make films it seems unlikely that they would want to make Westerns. They have their own stories.

3 passing as an indian

In the 1950s, contemporaneously with the stirrings that would lead to the Civil Rights movement and other manifestations of heightened racial consciousness, Hollywood made a series of films that were intended to present Indians in a sympathetic light. There's a certain air of deliberation about these films, an earnestness that springs from the knowledge of Hollywood's previous output, which had unthinkingly portrayed Indians as little more than mere obstacles to the onward march of progress across the continent. But the liberalism of these films did not extend to allowing Indians to portray themselves. If an Indian role was a leading part, then invariably it went to a white actor. In casting such roles Hollywood had a fixed idea of what it was looking for. In the case of the males, the actor should be tall, dark and handsome, but only in a certain manner, with looks that tended towards a certain gravitas, avoiding any suspicion of prettiness. He should be measured in his movements, and have a deep, resonant voice, speaking slowly. He should exude a kind of stoical dignity, his expression solemn but suggestive of a fierceness never far below the surface. In *Broken Arrow* (1950) Jeff Chandler played the Apache chief Cochise. In *Apache* (1954) Burt Lancaster played the lead role, while Robert Taylor was

Rock Hudson in Douglas Sirk's *Taza, Son of Cochise* (1953).

a Shoshone in *Devil's Doorway* (1950) and Rock Hudson played the title-role in *Taza, Son of Cochise* (1953). In all these films there is a real effort to redress the overt racism of many earlier Hollywood films, but no Indian actor was deemed able to carry the lead role. Indians had simply not acquired the star power believed necessary for the film's box-office success.

For female parts, casting directors often looked south of the border, to Europe or even further afield to fill Indian roles. Exoticism was in demand, a beauty which differed from the chocolate-box prettiness of Doris Day or Debbie Reynolds and which suggested the smouldering passion assumed to be the invariable possession of 'savage' people. Thus in *Across the Wide Missouri* (1950) the Indian companion of trapper Clark

Dolores del Rio as a Kiowa woman in Don Siegel's *Flaming Star* (1960).

Kirk Douglas and Elsa Martinelli in André de Toth's *The Indian Fighter* (1955).

Gable was played by Mexican-born Maria Elena Marques. Sarita Montiel, who played Rod Steiger's Sioux wife in *Run of the Arrow* (1957), was Spanish. In *Drum Beat* (1954) the Modoc girl, Toby, is played by Marisa Pavan, born in Sardinia. Playing another Sioux woman, opposite Kirk Douglas in *The Indian Fighter* (1955), was another Italian actress, Elsa Martinelli. Katy Jurado, also Mexican, played Spencer Tracy's Comanche wife in *Broken Lance* (1954) and the half-Apache Nita in *Arrowhead* (1953), while Audrey Hepburn, part English, part Dutch, played a Kiowa woman in *The Unforgiven* (1959). In *Geronimo* (1962) the Apache chief's wife Teela is played by Kamala Devi, born in Bombay.

The practice of casting women from other cultures and ethnic backgrounds continued well beyond the 1950s. Mexican-born Dolores Del Rio plays a Kiowa woman in *Flaming Star* (1960). In *Little Big Man* (1970), Dustin Hoffman's Cheyenne wife Sunshine is played by Aimée Eccles, a Chinese woman born in Hong Kong. As we have already seen, in *A Man Called Horse* (1970) Richard Harris's Sioux wife is played by a Greek, Corinna Tsopei. In a rare departure, in *The Big Sky* (1952) Howard Hawks cast unknown Elizabeth Threatt, whose mother was Cherokee, as a Blackfoot princess. It was her only film.

Doubtless producers at the time would have defended their casting on the grounds that sufficient competent Indian actors did not exist, although this is hardly surprising if Indians were never cast. But one suspects that casting a non-Indian woman of exotic appearance was a way of having one's cake and eating it too. The audience enjoyed the daring taboo attached to interracial sex, but was comforted by the knowledge that it was only make-believe.

Further down the cast list, Native American actors still struggled to find sizeable roles. John Ford was proud of his high standing among the Navajo people, yet he only ever used them as extras in his Westerns. The role of the Comanche chief Scar in *The Searchers* (1956), shot in Navajo country in Arizona, is played by Henry Brandon, born in Germany as Heinrich von Kleinbach. Brandon also played the Comanche Quanah Parker (an historical character, whose mother was a captive white woman) in Ford's *Two Rode Together* (1961). His opponent, fellow Comanche Stone Calf, is played by the black actor Woody Strode. Chief Red Shirt in *She Wore a Yellow Ribbon* (1949) is played by Noble Johnson, a black actor who in the silent era had set up the Lincoln Motion Picture Company to make black films for black audiences, but in later life played a series of minor Indian roles for Cecil B. DeMille.

Chief Big Tree as a scary Indian in John Ford's *Drums Along the Mohawk* (1939).

Dolores del Rio and Sal Mineo in John Ford's *Cheyenne Autumn* (1964).

On occasion Ford did use Indian actors: Chief Big Tree has a featured role in *Drums Along the Mohawk* (1939) and another one ten years later in *She Wore a Yellow Ribbon* (1949). But when Ford came to cast his last Western, *Cheyenne Autumn* (1964), intended as a kind of peace-offering to any Indians he might have offended with his earlier pictures, Ford cast in Cheyenne roles Sal Mineo (born in New York of Italian extraction), and Dolores del Rio, Ricardo Montalban and Gilbert Roland, all born in Mexico.

Indians, it seemed, could not become stars. Yet, para-doxically, the small number of Indian actors who managed to make a name for themselves in Westerns found that emphasizing their credentials by Indianizing their names improved their prospects. Jay Silverheels, born on the Six Nations reservation in Canada as Harold J. Smith, found fame as Tonto, the Lone Ranger's faithful companion in the long-running television series. Chief Thundercloud, who appeared frequently in Westerns from the 1930s to the '50s, had changed his name from Victor Daniels. Chief Big Tree was originally Isaac Johnny John. Hollywood was unwilling to allow Indians to carry the picture, but lower down the cast list it valued the seeming authenticity that genuine Indians could impart.

Jay Silverheels as Tonto with Clayton Moore as The Lone Ranger.

The best known of all Indian actors was Iron Eyes Cody, who made more than a hundred Westerns in a long career. He asserts in his autobiography, somewhat improbably, that though born in 1907 he appeared in two early D. W. Griffith Westerns, *Fighting Blood* (1911) and *The Massacre* (1912).[1] Cody also claims to have appeared in one of the most famous silent Westerns, *The Covered Wagon* (1923). Whatever his age when he started, he certainly made a lot of films, many routine but others more prestigious, such as Cecil B. DeMille's *Unconquered* (1947) and *Broken Arrow* (1950). Cody also played opposite Bob Hope in the classic Western comedy *The Paleface* (1948). According to the Internet Movie Database (www.imdb.com), the various Indian denominations he played included Arapaho, Apache, Sioux, Cherokee, Ute, Osage, Blackfoot and Shoshone.

One of Cody's biggest roles is in *Sitting Bull* (1954), in which he plays the Sioux warrior Crazy Horse (though the title role went to J. Carrol Naish, the descendant of a long line of Irish peers). The story is based loosely on the events leading up to the Battle of the Little Big Horn in 1876. Despite the title, Dale Robertson has the leading role in the film as a cavalry officer who takes the side of the Indians, who are being oppressed by a villainous Indian agent and by George Armstrong Custer. Eventually, after Custer's defeat, peace is restored through a face to face meeting between President Ulysses S. Grant and Sitting Bull (an event that occurred only in the imagination of the scriptwriters). In *Sitting Bull* Cody's role is to play the 'bad' Indian to Sitting Bull's good one. As such, wearing a succession of natty shirts, by turns pink, blue and buckskin (Cody gets a credit for 'Technical Adviser and Indian Costumes'), he continually calls for war against the whites, while Sitting Bull urges restraint. When at the conclusion of the battle Crazy Horse wants to scalp Custer, Sitting Bull forbids it. Cody's performance, though not without vigour, lacks light and shade. 'Kill, kill!' is his constant refrain.

At one point Iron Eyes Cody is given a speech that pre-echoes his later fame as a spokesman for the ecological movement. Gold is discovered in the Black Hills and miners flood in, killing Indians. 'And now another kind [of white man] comes – this one wants gold,' says Crazy Horse. 'He kills game he cannot eat, he fouls the clear water.' Towards the end of his

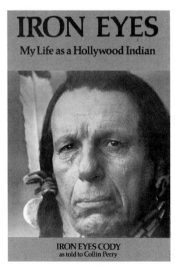

The cover of Iron Eyes Cody's 1984 autobiography.

career Cody achieved iconic status when he appeared in a TV commercial for the environmental agency Keep America Beautiful. Cody paddles an Indian canoe down a river polluted with garbage. The assumption is that as the first custodians of the land, Indians kept it clean and pure. At the end there is a close-up of Cody shedding a tear for what has been done to America's natural beauty; this image is used on the cover of his autobiography, and the ad is still available on the internet.[2] Building on his career in movies and on the fame that this commercial gave him, Cody went on to be a kind of roving ambassador for Indian peoples, and his autobiography includes photographs of him shaking hands with Presidents Jimmy Carter and Ronald Reagan and with Pope John Paul.

With the benefit of hindsight, he does not look particularly Indian, with his long bony face and big nose. Shortly before Cody died, Angela Aleiss, a PhD student at UCLA, began to research into Cody's background. In his autobiography he states that his mother was a Cree and his father, Thomas Longplume Cody, a Cherokee who appeared with Buffalo Bill's Wild West travelling show.[3] Aleiss discovered that this Indian heritage was a complete fabrication, and that Cody was in fact born Oscar DeCorti in Louisiana in 1904. Both his parents were immigrants from southern Italy. Far from his father having worked with Buffalo Bill, he deserted his young family in 1909 and his wife never saw him again. Cody himself never acknowledged any of the falsifications of his background, nor, curiously, did some of his Indian friends. Aleiss published her researches in an article in the New Orleans

Times-Picayune but her revelations attracted little attention at the time.[4] At Cody's death in 1999, authoritative sources were still reproducing Cody's own version of his life story. It didn't give me much pleasure to write to the *Guardian* correcting their obituary, which was largely taken at face value from Cody's autobiography, since *The BFI Companion to the Western*, first published in 1988 and edited by me, had also swallowed Cody's story whole.[5]

To this day the website www.ironeyescody.com still maintains that Cody was a Cherokee. Bonnie Paradise, former executive director of the American Indian Registry of the Performing Arts, declared that Cody 'lived and breathed an Indian lifestyle. In that sense, at least, no one can call him an impostor.' Kathleen Whitaker, chief curator of the Southwest Museum, where Cody's wife Bertha worked, remarked: 'What difference does it make? Iron Eyes brought forth the true essence of what being American Indian is all about.'[6] It's a testament to the overwhelming power of our preconceptions about Indians, our need to believe in the myths we have created, that someone who was not Indian at all can be seen as even more Indian than the real thing. For what real Native American could claim to actually be 'the true essence' of the Indian?

Is it good enough to say that Cody's personal origins don't matter just so long as he represented all that was best in the Indian? In telling his own story he frequently claims to be an authority on Indian customs and practices. Thus he takes pleasure in recounting an argument with Cecil B. DeMille over the authenticity of the Indian costumes for *The Plainsman*

(1936).[7] Likewise, Cody presents himself as a skilled practitioner of Indian sign language. In the episode devoted to the Western in Kevin Brownlow's television history *Hollywood*, Cody, in resplendent Indian costume, says that the great silent Western actor William S. Hart got his sign language wrong. But is Cody any more reliable a guide? His white employers wanted to believe his claims about his ancestry and so were willing to listen to his opinions. But would a government agency such as Keep America Beautiful have employed him to make their commercial if they had known the truth about his origins?

There is a nicely sardonic comment on the Iron Eyes affair in an episode of *The Sopranos*.[8] Some Indians are holding a protest against Columbus Day on the grounds that celebrating the achievements of the 'discoverer' of America is disrespectful to those who suffered in consequence. Tony and the boys are annoyed at this insult to a famous Italian, and make the counter-charge that Iron Eyes Cody was an Italian too. From the opposite perspective, two Indian novelists have put their own gloss on Cody's career. In *Green Grass, Running Water* Thomas King gives a brief career resumé of Portland, the father of one of his characters, who had gone to Hollywood to play Indian extras in Westerns (interestingly, the novel was first published in 1993, three years before Aleiss published her revelations about Cody's ethnic origins):

Portland and Lillian sat around one night with CB [described elsewhere as 'a red-headed Italian who played some of the Indian leads'] and his wife, Isabella, and drank wine and tried to think of the most absurd name they could imagine.

'Iron Eyes Screeching Eagle. It still makes me laugh.'

But before the year was out, Portland was playing chiefs. He played Quick Fox in *Duel at Sioux Crossing*, Chief Jumping Otter in *They Rode for Glory*, and Chief Lazy Dog in *Cheyenne Sunrise* [all apocryphal titles]. He was a Sioux eighteen times, a Cheyenne ten times, a Kiowa six times, an Apache five times, and a Navaho once.

'We were on top of the world then. We lived in an apartment that had a pink swimming pool. Can you imagine? And if you stood on the toilet, you could see the ocean.'

'Did you know any of the big movie stars?'

'All of them,' Charlie's mother told him. 'We knew them all.'

'So what happened? Why'd you leave Hollywood?'

Lillian had Charlie sit very close to her and said in a whisper that Charlie could barely hear, 'It was his nose, Charlie.' And she laughed, the effort sending spasms through her thin body. 'It was your father's nose that brought us home.'[9]

In *Dark River* (1999), by Louis Owens, one of the characters, Shorty Luke, has also spent time in Hollywood. His reminiscences make a wry comment on Cody's Italian ancestry:

Shorty Luke had been given the cat, which he called
Mingo, by a famous Hollywood actor named Iron Eyes
Cody when he'd gone back for a stunt man's big party
only three or four years earlier . . . He'd shown everyone a photograph of the very old Indian actor holding
the kitten. Domingo had thought the actor's black hair
was floating half an inch above his white scalp and very
wrinkled face. The man looked like he had makeup on.
He'd said as much but Shorty had glared. 'That man's
rich and famous,' he'd said. 'He's been in three
hundred movies.'

'That's a lot of times to fall off your horse,' Jessie
had interjected. 'That could definitely raise your hair.'

"Me and him and Sal Mineo used to eat lunch
together,' Shorty insisted . . . 'Sal didn't speak good Italian like some of the other actors . . . I think he was self-
conscious about not speaking Italian as well as most of
the other Indians. You know how it is.'[10]

Cody was not the only one living a lie. The early silent
film actress Mona Darkfeather (1882–1977) appeared in
several Westerns playing Indian roles, and the publicity put
out by Thomas Ince's Bison studio referred to her as a full-
blooded Blackfoot. In a magazine interview in 1914 she
conceded that this was stretching things. Instead, she claimed:

'My parents are descended from an aristocratic Spanish
family who came to this country many years back. I was

born in Los Angeles and have lived here nearly all my life. I was educated at a Catholic school in this city.' 'Spanish and not Sioux,' I sighed. 'Yes, too bad, isn't it?' Mona's tone was sympathetic but there was sarcasm in those brilliant black eyes of hers, 'however, I am an Indian Princess, for I was made a blood member of the Blackfoot Indians and given the title of "Princess" by Chief Big Thunder. I feel half Indian anyway, for I have lived among them so much and I speak several Indian languages and understand poor Lo as few people do.'[11]

Yet even this was not the truth, for the actress's real name was Josephine Workman; she was the daughter of a prominent southern Californian Anglo family, first established in the Los Angeles area in the 1840s, and whose house now forms part of the Homestead Museum.[12] A somewhat more complicated case was that of Long Lance or, to give him the full name he aspired to, Chief Buffalo Child Long Lance. He was the star of a feature-length documentary-style film called *Silent Enemy*, released in 1930. It tells the story of a group of Ojibwa Indians and their hunt for food as they struggle against hunger, the 'silent enemy' of the title. Much was made by the producers, W. Douglas Burden and William C. Chanler, of the authenticity of their film, which claimed to pay close attention to costume and customs in recreating scenes of Indian life from the age before the whites arrived. No matter that the leading Indians hired to re-enact these scenes were drawn from a variety of different Indian nationalities, none of them Ojibwa; the presence of real Indians would serve to legitimate the spectacle being offered.

Long Lance was promoted as a full-blooded member of the Blackfoot tribe. But before the film could be released it was claimed that he was in fact a black man, born Sylvester Long in Winston-Salem, North Carolina. As Nancy Cook has shown, this claim is somewhat misleading, since Long's ancestry was in the Lumbee community, who although regarded by some as blacks, nevertheless insist to this day on their Indian heritage and are still petitioning the US Government for formal recognition of their status as an Indian tribe. It seems likely that if Long had black ancestors he also had Indian ones, and could therefore lay justifiable claim to Indian heritage. Whatever Long's true origins, the producers tried to keep them secret, fearing the scandal would damage the film's prospects, but after its release Long dropped out of the public eye and died soon after, possibly murdered, some suggested, by the husband of a white woman whose lover he was.[13]

It may seem surprising that within Hollywood, despite its being prone to blurring the distinction between reality and fiction, whites should seek to pass themselves off as Indians. Cultural makeovers were not uncommon, but usually they involved actors attempting to disguise their ethnic origins if they lay outside the confines of a WASP heritage. Thus Jewish actors such as Kirk Douglas and Tony Curtis felt obliged to change their names from Issur Danielovitch and Bernard Schwartz. Clearly there was something different at stake with those such as Iron Eyes Cody. In *Playing Indian* Philip Deloria explores the long and intriguing history of white people in North America dressing up as Indians. The men who attacked ships carrying British property during the Boston Tea Party in 1773 were disguised as Indians, and their costume symbolized a state of wildness and rebellion. In the nineteenth century, as Indians themselves came under increasing threat from white expansion, secret societies of whites such as the Society of Red Men and Lewis Henry Morgan's New Confederacy of the Iroquois were formed as repositories of Indian lore and traditions, with rituals supposedly copied from the Iroquois and other tribes.[14] In the early twentieth century Ernest Thompson Seton founded the Woodcraft Indians, an organization for boys that tried to harness the supposed primitive qualities of Indian culture as a means of reinvigorating American youth, enervated by the softness of modern living. The boys were organized into '"tribes," camped in tipis, donned feather headdresses, "scalped" each other (one's "scalp", a tuft of horsehair, could be lost in competitive games), counted coup, and smoked peace pipes.[15] A parallel organization, the Camp Fire Girls, all too predictably placed its emphasis not on putting young girls in touch with their inner primitive but on developing home-making skills; as Charlotte Gulick, one of the founders, put it:

> The bearing and rearing of children has always been the first duty of most women, and that must always continue to be. This involves service, constant service, self-forgetfulness, and always service. I suggest the fire be taken as the symbol of the girls' movement, the

domestic fire – not the wild fire – and that from the first the very meaning of the fire be explained to her in poetry and dance.[16]

In the 1950s organizations offering adult whites an experience of Indian life were springing up all over America (and, as we shall see, in Europe too). Deloria interprets the widespread phenomenon of Indian hobbyists, whites who spend their weekends and summer holidays dressing up and playing at Indians, as a search for authenticity and closeness to nature and the forces of the primitive world, believed lacking in contemporary middle-class existence in the middle of the century:

> A glance round the cultural landscape revealed, on the one hand, high living standards, happy nuclear families, shiny advertising, proud patriotism, and a feeling of national consensus boosted by powerful social and political institutions. On the other hand, one also found a dark sense of alienation, middle-class citizens constantly suspecting a dry rot beneath their cheerful veneer. If America looked to some like a land of liberty and sunshine, for others it was a world of McCarthyite paranoia, deep racial tension, and hysteria in the face of rock and roll, comic books, and teen delinquency.[17]

The magazine of the movement, *American Indian Hobbyist*, later *American Indian Tradition*, was founded in

1954. It acted as a focus for all those who sought to be put in touch with the something deeper, the something more 'real' that Indian life promised. As the 1950s gave way to the '60s and '70s, playing Indian became a major component of the emerging hippie lifestyle and the subsequent New Age movement. Prominent in such thinking was a growing awareness of ecological issues, and increasingly Indians came to be seen as having a special relationship to the earth and uniquely qualified to preserve it. Real-life Indians might be stuck at the bottom of the heap economically and socially: one-third of Indians on the reservations live below the poverty line, rates of alcoholism are often higher than 50 per cent, on some reservations unemployment is above 80 per cent, and barely 7 per cent of Indians graduate from college, half the national rate. But the idea of 'Indianness' has maintained its high cultural prestige. Passing as an Indian is for some more than a matter of keeping an eye on the main chance.

Such ethnic mobility has not been confined to the movies. Grey Owl was the author of a number of bestselling books published in the 1930s, including *Tales from an Empty Cabin* (1936). For many years Grey Owl had worked for the Canadian parks service, and his books drew on both his long experience of living in the wild and his heritage as an Apache Indian. His publications made him famous and he embarked on a series of speaking tours, preaching his message of care for the environment based on a traditional Indian lifestyle. But though his knowledge of how to live in the wilderness may have been real enough, his claim to be Indian was pure inven-

Grey Owl.

tion. Grey Owl had been born Archibald Belaney in Hastings, England, where he had been brought up by two elderly aunts before emigrating to Canada in 1906. In the course of the next thirty years he formed a number of relationships with Indian women, one of whom, Anahareo, of Mohawk extraction, encouraged him to begin his writing career. Alcohol abuse contributed greatly to his early death at the age of 50 in 1938; only then was the secret of his origins revealed to the public. In 1999 a feature film of his life, entitled simply *Grey Owl*, was released, directed by Richard Attenborough and starring Pierce Brosnan. Reminiscent of the manner in which some of Iron Eyes Cody's Indian friends refused publicly to acknowledge his non-Indian birth, towards the end of the film Grey Owl goes to an Indian pow wow somewhat nervous in case the chiefs, who know of his masquerade, reject him. But they all laugh, making light of his fears. 'Men become what they dream', says one old chief. 'You have dreamed well.'[18]

Another case of an Englishman masquerading as an Indian is described in Linda Colley's book *Captives*, which studies the experience of hundreds of British people captured in North Africa, North America and India over several centuries. Peter Williamson, who was born in Scotland in 1730, was indentured in America and then taken captive by Indians in Pennsylvania for a period of several months. After he escaped and returned to Britain, he published several narratives of his life. In each one he embroidered his narrative until finally in 1789 he claimed that he had actually been reared from childhood by his Delaware captors, which had given him a profound understanding of the Indian way of life.[19]

Much more recently, we can note in passing the strange case of Jamake Highwater, who, born around 1930, was adopted and brought up as Jay Marks near Los Angeles. In his twenties he became involved in contemporary dance and music, becoming a choreographer and writer about cultural matters. The American Indian Movement's occupation of Alcatraz in 1969 apparently persuaded Marks that he had Indian ancestry and so he changed his name to Jamake Highwater and began to write both fiction and non-fiction books about Indian matters. But there were persistent charges that his Indian ancestry was false, one accuser even bizarrely claiming that Highwater was in fact the experimental film-maker Gregory Markopoulos.[20]

More widely known is the case of Sacheen Little-feather, who appeared on stage at the Oscars ceremony in 1973 on behalf of Marlon Brando to refuse his award for Best Actor in *The Godfather*. According to a speech that she delivered on Brando's behalf, 'the motion picture community as much as anyone has been responsible for degrading the Indian.' This seems no more than a bald statement of the truth but outraged the great and the good of Hollywood. Littlefeather appeared in full Indian regalia and claimed to be an Apache. Subsequent investigations showed that her real name was Maria Cruz and she was of mixed Apache, Yaqui, Pueblo and Caucasian heritage. Prior to her appearance at the Oscars she had a few minor film roles and had been voted Miss American Vampire; she subsequently appeared nude in *Playboy*, but claimed that the FBI ruined her film career. Littlefeather/Cruz may not have been quite who she said she was, but hardly deserved the snide remarks uttered at the time by actors such as Clint Eastwood, John Wayne and Michael Caine.[21]

Why should all these people (and there have been many others) risk the shame of exposure by basing a career as an Indian on deception? In some cases the motive is not hard to find. On 7 June 2004 the *Guardian* reported the case of Ronald Roberts, who claimed to be Sachem Golden Eagle, leader of the Western Mohegans. Many Indian tribes have made money by building casinos on their reservations, which are not subject to federal laws about gambling. Roberts, a former travelling evangelist and country and western singer, attempted to defraud investors by setting up a casino on land he argued belonged to a tribe he had in fact invented. To an extent, though far less culpably, others who have passed for Indians have also been motivated by money, gaining fame and fortune because those who controlled the white media, whether cinema or publishing, believed that their Indianness made them saleable, that their Indian identity provided them with their unique selling point. Hollywood in particular, the 'dream factory' whose stock-in-trade was the creation of illusions, needed constantly to anchor its fabrications in some sort of reality. Indian actors could lend the Western, a genre that clung however precariously to a kind of historical foundation, a guarantee of authenticity.

If until late in the twentieth century Indian actors were not regarded as having sufficient star-power to carry a picture, lower down the cast list they could offer some reinforcement of the truth-claims of a film. No matter that Indian actors were usually cast to represent tribes quite other than the one they owed their origins to. What did the producers, or the audience, care that Chief Big Tree, playing a member of the Arapaho, a plains tribe, in *She Wore a Yellow Ribbon*, was in fact a Seneca Indian, people who were part of the Iroquois federation of tribes situated in the north-east of the United States? As far as Hollywood was concerned, differences between Indian peoples were insignificant; seen one Indian, you've seen 'em all. To Indians, however, this must have seemed as strange as if a Chinese filmmaker, requiring an actor to play a Spaniard, should recruit a Norwegian, on the grounds that both countries are part of Europe.

Yet undoubtedly something more than money was at stake for many of those who passed as Indians. One does not hear of white actors trying to pass as blacks or as Chinese, and the reason, one suspects, is not merely the physical barriers to doing so, since after all 'white' people come in a wide variety of physical types. (The question of blacks or other ethnic groups trying to pass for white is a separate issue, in which the motivation, to escape social prejudice, is patent. Hollywood made several films on just this phenomenon, for example Elia Kazan's *Pinky* (1949) and Douglas Sirk's *Imitation of Life* (1959), at the time of the wave of liberal films about Indians.) It's the idea of Indian culture, or rather what whites conceive as Indian culture, that makes people want to cross the racial divide. According to a certain conception, which has its intellectual roots in Rousseau's notion of 'the noble savage', Indians are straightforward, dignified, brave and, in general, uncorrupted by civilization. Especially, and this is a theme that seems to pre-date the modern environmental movement, they are the custodians of the natural world, instinctive guardians of its resources and its beauty. Thus Grey Owl's writings emphasize the pristine beauty of the lakes and woods, and Iron Eyes grieves for the despoliation of his land.

Perhaps the best known of Indian environmentalists is the Indian leader Seattle, chief of the Suquamish people, who is supposed to have delivered a speech in Washington Territory in 1854 in response to the Americans who were trying to buy his people's land. The speech was in fact not recorded until 1887, by a white doctor, Henry Smith, who claimed to have been present when it was delivered. Much later, the speech was rewritten by Ted Perry for a documentary film in 1972. It reads in part:

> Every part of this earth is sacred to my people.
>
> Every shining pine needle, every sandy shore, every mist in the dark woods, every clearing and humming insect is holy in the memory and experience of my people. The sap which courses through the trees carries the memories of the red man.
>
> The white man's dead forget the country of their birth when they go to walk among the stars. Our dead never forget this beautiful earth, for it is the mother of the red man.
>
> We are part of the earth and it is part of us.
>
> The perfumed flowers are our sisters; the deer, the horse, the great eagle, these are our brothers.

Despite Perry's protest that the version he produced was never intended to be understood as Seattle's exact words, the speech, treated as an authentic, verbatim document of Indian ecological awareness, was reproduced in a children's book, *Brother Eagle, Sister Sky: A Message from Chief Seattle*, which went on to become a bestseller and win a prestigious book award. It is still in print.[22] Part of Seattle's speech was quoted in a book by Vice-President Al Gore, *Earth in the Balance*, as well as by dozens of environmental organizations, and these apocryphal words have gone down as the single most-quoted statement on Indian environmental beliefs. Clearly, whatever the chief may or may not have said, very many people want strongly to believe in the environmental credentials of Indian people.

That Indians were ecologically minded is to some extent a myth. Plains Indians regularly killed buffalo in their hundreds by stampeding them over a cliff, producing more meat than they could use. Indians actively assisted white trappers in hunting beaver and other fur-bearing animals down to levels that threatened their survival.[23] There is evidence that some early Indian cultures died out through unsustainable agricultural and environmental practices.[24] Some present-day Indian tribes have actively campaigned to have nuclear waste dumps sited on their land, just for the money it would bring in. If the effects of Indians on the environment were far less destructive than those later perpetuated by whites, this may be because there were fewer of them and because they did not have the technology to destroy on such a large scale. Moreover, having established their civilization in a particular form, whether small-scale farming, fishing in rivers or hunting, their interests were in preserving and conserving, not in transforming the environment into something else. Never-

Chief Dan George.

theless, the idea that Indians were and are by nature environmentalists still persists.

Since the 1970s Hollywood has made slow progress towards accepting Indian actors in leading parts. One who achieved considerable prominence in a couple of high-profile Westerns was Chief Dan George. Born in 1899 on a reservation in Vancouver, and according to some sources originally named Geswanouth Slahoot, he did not become an actor until over sixty years of age, receiving an Academy Award nomination for the role of Old Lodge Skins, the wise and wily Indian who adopts Jack Crabb (Dustin Hoffman) in *Little Big Man* (1970). Thomas Berger's novel, on which the film is based, brought a welcome touch of humour to the portrayal of Indians, who previously had been conceived as solemn, stony-faced and statuesque. Neither the book nor the film is inclined to be overly reverential about Indian ecological habits, Jack Crabb observing that on approaching an Indian camp one is moved to remark, on seeing the rubbish strewn about, 'I see their dump, but where is the camp?' Yet in general Indian life is presented as innately superior to that of the whites, sexually more tolerant and less hypocritical, and more in touch with the natural world and spiritual matters. It's essentially a flower-power vision of the Indian, produced at the time when the 'New Age' philosophy of the hippy movement was attempting to assimilate Indian culture.

Chief Dan George's other major role was as the displaced Indian Lone Waite in Clint Eastwood's *The Outlaw Josey Wales* (1976). Waite is a Cherokee, a member of one of the so-called Five Civilized Tribes, who has an amusing if rueful take on the white view of his people: 'They call us civilized because we're easy to sneak up on.' Josey, the hero of the film, a victimized Confederate played by Eastwood, befriends Waite and eventually comes to live in harmony with his Comanche neighbours surrounding the refuge he has found in the west. Their chief, Ten Bears, is played by the Creek Indian actor Will Sampson.

This pro-Indian film is based on a novel, *Gone to Texas*, written under the name of Forrest Carter, and originally published in 1973 under the title *The Rebel Outlaw: Josey Wales*. In 1976 Carter published another book, *The Education of Little Tree*, which claimed to be an autobiography and in which he tells of his upbringing as a part-Cherokee boy. Full of notions about the innate understanding of nature demonstrated by indigenous peoples, it constructs a sympathetic if patronizing view of the childlike simplicity of Indian ways. It's surprising, then, that the author turned out to be another in the lengthening list of those who have passed for an Indian. In truth, Forrest Carter was Asa Carter, a white supremacist, an anti-Semite, a member of the Ku Klux Klan, and a speechwriter for George Wallace, the segregationist governor of Alabama. How he squared these views in his own mind with his pro-Indian fiction is difficult to say, but Shari M. Huhndorf has argued that in *The Education of Little Tree* Carter effects a subtle but distorted version of history to suit his disguised racist ends. Thus in a central sequence Little Tree is put into a white school, where he is badly mistreated; eventually he is withdrawn from the school to go back to the woods and live happily with his grandfather. This segregation, it is implied, is a good thing, since integration only leads to the ostracism of the minority race. Carter tries to identify the Cherokee (who were removed by whites from their ancestral lands) with the defeated Confederates, in particular the mountain folk leading a life close to nature in the backwoods. Both lead a primitive, pre-industrial existence, resistant to the industrialized northern Yankees and to the government, which has dispossessed them. The Indians, however, despite their attractive qualities, are conceptualized in both books through a form of social Darwinism, in which the survival of the fittest means that inevitably they must give way to the whites. In this view, with the ultimate disappearance of the Indians, the southern whites become the natural inheritors of the land. In the film of *The Outlaw Josey Wales* the Comanche with whom the hero makes his peace eventually fade away, to leave him in possession of their territory.[25]

In the 1990s genuine Indians were at last allowed to play major leading roles. As we have seen, Indian actors fill major roles in *Dances With Wolves* (1990). Wes Studi, a Cherokee from Oklahoma, has a non-speaking role as a Pawnee in this film, and was then elevated to play the major role of Magua in *The Last of the Mohicans* (1992) and the title-role in *Geronimo: An American Legend* (1994). Russell Means, a Sioux, played the important part of Chingachgook in *Last of the Mohicans* and has continued to work regularly in movies. Eric Schweig, of Inuit origin, played Chingachgook's son Uncas, and has had a dozen roles since. One could hardly say that Indian actors are prominent in contemporary cinema. But it's a lot less likely that a major Indian character would now be played by a white actor, or that any white actor would seek to masquerade as a genuine Indian. Though given the persistence of this syndrome one can never be sure.

4 indians in the european western

The American West is, one might say, a European invention. The first white men to explore it were Europeans – French, Spanish, Britons – and it would be well over two centuries before any white men who set foot into the wilderness would think of themselves as Americans. If Europeans had not already been gripped by a fantasy about the West, one that drew them across the ocean and into unexplored lands, then the western part of North America might never have become part of the United States.

The first representations of the indigenous inhabitants of America were also made by Europeans, for example Jacques Le Moyne's pictures of Florida Indians in 1564 and John White's drawings in Virginia in 1585–7. Written accounts began to appear very soon after Columbus's discoveries, and indeed the great explorer himself, an Italian working for the Spanish, wrote down his impressions, among which was that the Indians, as he mistakenly called them, knew 'neither sect nor idolatry, with the exception that all believe that the source of all power and goodness is in the sky.'[1] A mere dozen years after Columbus's first landing, European writers were already summarizing the character of the peoples newly discovered, with a mixture of observation and wild surmise that was to

Engraving after a watercolour drawing of an Indian made by John White in Virginia, 1585–6.

become familiar, as in this description published in Germany in 1505:

> The people are thus naked, handsome, brown, well-formed in body, their heads, necks, arms, privy parts, feet of women and men are slightly covered with feathers. The men also have many precious stones in their faces and breasts. No one owns anything but all things are in common. And the men have as wives those that please them, be they mothers, sisters or friends, therein

they make no difference. They also fight with each other. They also eat each other even those that are slain, and hang the flesh of them in smoke. They live one hundred and fifty years. And have no government.[2]

From the earliest times, it seems, European views of Indians were polarized. Indians were either devils or angels, on the one hand engaging in cannibalism and sexual promiscuity (doubtless a projection of the Europeans' own fantasies), and on the other living a life of bliss untrammelled by the burdens of civilization. As one writer put it at the beginning of the sixteenth century, the Indians 'seem to live in that golden world of which old writers speak so much, wherein men lived simply and innocently without enforcement of laws, without quarrelling, judges and libels, content only to satisfy nature.'[3] In the eighteenth century this latter view was elaborated into the concept of the Noble Savage, given a philosophical underpinning by Jean-Jacques Rousseau in his *Discourse on the Origin of Inequality among Men* (1755), which argued that Indians were morally superior to Europeans because they had not been corrupted by wealth and the other trappings of modern society. This idealization of the Indians served a political purpose, as the supposed superiority of the Indians was used as a stick to beat the present state of European society and its political structures, particularly in pre-revolutionary France.

The idea of the Noble Savage was brought to full flower by the ensuing Romantic movement. *Atala* (1801), a novel by François René, vicomte de Chateaubriand, has as its hero the Natchez chief Chactas, who, captured by Seminoles, is threatened with death by torture, only to be rescued by the beautiful mixed-race Atala. She is a Christian and helps Chactas to safety at a Christian mission. They fall deeply in love but the next morning Chactas finds that she has taken poison. Having vowed to her mother to remain a virgin, Atala has been unnerved that she might succumb to Chactas's charms and so has taken her own life. Chateaubriand's Indians owe nothing to the real world, but are instead creatures of a dreamy imagination, ethereal figures whose hair is 'veils of gold' and who are 'as sweet as the plants on which they were nourished'.[4] *Atala* was extraordinarily successful, and the image of the grieving Chactas, the epitome of the melancholy Romantic hero pining for an impossible love, took on iconic status in a series of pictures and statues, including etchings made by Gustave Doré for an edition in 1863. Undoubtedly such fanciful images of the Indians were only sustainable by those who were far removed from day-to-day experience of them; Chateaubriand had spent a mere five months in America, a full decade before he wrote his book. Later European authors were often willing to let their imaginations roam unencumbered by even a solitary visit.

The concept of the Noble Savage and his alter-ego, the cruel and cunning Indian, served two opposing functions for nineteenth-century Europeans. On the one hand, Indians roaming the open prairie, untrammelled by the irksome bonds of established and authoritarian society, offered a vision of freedom to a continent for the most part still trying to shake off the shackles of feudalism. On the other hand, Europeans could thrill themselves with stories of Indian savagery while remaining safe in their beds. Both concepts are found at work in the novels of James Fenimore Cooper. In his best-known story, *The Last of the Mohicans* (1826), Cooper contrasts good Indians, Chingachgook and his son Uncas, brave friends of the white hero, with the evil Magua. Cooper became immensely popular in Europe, his novels being translated into virtually every European language; 32 of his collected works had appeared in Russia before the revolution, for example. His novels were also frequently dramatized for the stage. Europeans were not slow to imitate his work, but few attempted to match Cooper's literary ambitions. Almost all the European fiction written about the American West in the nineteenth century took the form of popular pot-boilers with little claim to literary quality. In France Gustave Aimard's turgid *Les Trappeurs de l'Arkansas* (1858) was a bestseller and soon translated into English. In Britain, Mayne Reid's *The Scalp Hunters; or, Romantic Adventures in Northern Mexico* (1851) was a lurid account of endless bloody battles against Apaches.

Ray Allen Billington has given an entertaining account of Indians appearing in popular European fiction of the nineteenth century. The idea of the noble savage exerted a powerful hold on the imagination. Thus Indians were often described as having classical good looks; a Norwegian author writes of an Apache so striking 'he would make Apollo envious', while his Comanche adversary 'presented the most perfect build a sculptor could have dreamed of'.[5] They speak in a highly stylized and poetic manner: 'You left the village of the Flowers', an Apache chief remarks in a French novel, 'to follow the hunting path at daybreak of the third sun of the moon of the falling leaves; thirty suns have passed since that period, and we are hardly at the moon of the passing game.'[6] The women are all beautiful and dressed in the most exquisite costumes. A French author describes White Gazelle, a Comanche princess, clad in 'loose Turkish trousers made of Indian cashmere, fastened at the knee with diamond garters . . . a jacket of violet velvet buttoned over the bosom with a profusion of diamonds . . . a brilliant-hued Navajo zarape and a Panama hat of extreme fineness decorated with an eagle plume.'[7] The Indians of the Southwest are described as inhabiting fantastic palaces two hundred feet high, and their temples decorated with precious stones. Their leaders are unsurpassed in their knowledge of military tactics, often gleaned from a study of Napoleon.[8]

At the same time, these authors perpetuated the division between good and bad Indians. For example, good Indians are merciful in victory, but bad Indians engage in the most hideous tortures. A British author describes with lip-smacking relish the torture of a Sioux by his Chippewa captors. They light a fire on his stomach, after which 'His tongue lolled out of his mouth. A horrid smell arose from the charred flesh . . . which could be heard crackling under the heat.' After being used as a target for knife-throwing, the victim has a thong tightened about his head till his eyeballs stick out, then one of his torturers takes a knife and 'scooped out the eyeballs and threw them on the ground. First the right eye, then the left.'[9]

The sheer volume of the output of such writings in this period, mainly fictional, is testament to the Europeans' fascination with the West and with Indians in particular. Perhaps the most extraordinary and influential of these novelists was the German Karl May. A convicted criminal who spent several years in prison for fraud, he began writing on his release in 1874. In the 1880s May churned out a series of novels set in the American West, including *Winnetou* (1893), *Old Surehand* (1894) and *Der Schatz im Silbersee* (*The Treasure of Silver Lake*, 1894). The books recount the adventures of his white hero, a German who goes under the name of Old

Cover of the 1893 edition of Karl May's *Winnetou*.

Shatterhand, and his companion Winnetou, an Apache who has all the noble instincts of Cooper's Mohicans and shares their melancholy foreboding of impending decline. Together they roam the West, upsetting the dastardly schemes of villainous Yankees, Mormons and less noble Indians.

The huge success of these novels (it has been estimated that more than 100 million copies of Karl May's books have been sold in Germany)[10] went to the author's head, and increasingly he claimed that they were based on personal experience. Eventually this was exposed as a lie (May did not visit America until 1908, and even then got no further West than Chicago). At this time his criminal past was also revealed to his public, but although this damaged his reputation with the guardians of culture, he has remained a favourite of generations of German-speaking readers. Among those who devoured his works were Albert Einstein and Adolf Hitler, who, according to the diaries of Albert Speer, was a great admirer and derived justification in May's lack of direct experience of his subject matter for his own assumption of command of troops fighting in foreign lands: 'it was not necessary to know the desert in order to direct troops in the African theater of war', Hitler argued. 'It wasn't necessary to travel in order to know the world.'[11] Hitler allegedly ordered his generals to read *Winnetou* after the defeat at Stalingrad.[12]

May was not alone in his endeavours. Several other German writers of the period attained great success with adventure stories set in the Wild West, and more than a thousand fictional Indian stories were published in Germany

Karl May in 1907.

between 1875 and 1900.[13] Prominent among nineteenth-century German authors was Charles Sealsfield (1793–1864), whose *Tokeah; or, The White Rose*, published in English before its German publication in 1833, recounts the story of Tokeah, a Cherokee chief trying to resist white incursions into his lands. Sealsfield follows the agenda of contemporary American administrations in his belief that the Indians were ultimately doomed and that their forced removal from their lands was the only way to preserve what was left of their culture.[14] Friedrich Gerstäcker (1816–1872), author of *Flusspiraten des Mississippi* (*River Pirates of the Mississippi*, 1848), had spent some time living with Indians and, though he believed they were ultimately to perish, argued in his novels 'how appallingly often have the Indians really been treated most contemptibly by people who knew nothing sacred in the world and openly stated that they would be as pleased to shoot an Indian as a wolf.'[15] Another prolific writer, Balduin Möllhausen (1825–1905), sometimes called 'the German Cooper', was the author of *Der Halbindianer* (*The Halfbreed*, 1861), about a man whose Indian and white heritage are perpetually at war with each other.

Unlike May, all these German writers had some direct experience of the American West and of Indians. But it was May who created the most powerful and enduring mythology of the Indian for German readers. Winnetou is a charismatic figure of impressive appearance. Old Shatterhand records his first impressions:

> His moccasins were embellished with porcupine quills, and his leather jacket with patterns of red stitching. Like his father, he carried a knife and double-barrelled rifle, and his medicine bag hung from a beaded leather thong. His head was also uncovered and displayed no feather, but the long blue-black hair cascading down his back was interlaced with snakeskin. His features, even nobler than his father's, were unlined, the skin a dull light brown with bronze highlights. His height was the same as mine, and as I later learned, our ages also matched.[16]

Winnetou proves to be a man of rare culture, speaking perfect English and High German, ending every speech with the words 'Howgh, ich habe gesprochen'. To this the other

Indians answer 'Uff, uff', rendered in the English translation as 'Ugh, ugh'. He has been educated by a white man who has been living with the Apache for many years, and who has introduced Winnetou to the best of American authors. Old Shatterhand comes across the Apache chief in his camp:

> He was wearing a white linen robe, and carried no weapons. A book was under his arm, and I could read part of the title '– OF HIAWATHA' in gold letters. This son of the 'savage' race of Indians could not only read, but had a taste for classic literature, in this case Longfellow's epic poem celebrating noble and romantic characteristics of his race. Poetry in the hands of an Apache Indian![17]

Winnetou has a sister, Nisho-chi, beautiful, of course:

> She wore a long gown, belted at the waist with a snake-skin, but no jewelry at all, no silver or turquoise like many Indians commonly wear . . . Her sole decoration was luxuriant blue-black hair, falling in two glistening braids to her waist. It reminded me of Winnetou's, and her features were also similar to his. The same velvet-black eyes under long, heavy lashes, soft full cheeks and a dimpled chin, her skin a pale copper-bronze with silver highlights.[18]

Inevitably, Old Shatterhand falls for this maiden, but in a manner similar to that of many interracial love affairs in

Western movies, for example *Broken Arrow*, the romance is doomed, Nisho-chi being killed before they can marry. Clearly the real love affair is between the German *Westmann* and the Apache chief with the velvet-black eyes.

May's book is full of frontier lore and ethnographic detail intended to lend authenticity:

> The 'medicine bag' of the Southwest Indian tribes has little to do with *medicine*, nor with the 'medicine bundles' of other tribes. The word was taken from the white man's language to describe the Indian equivalent of the palefaces' magic powers. The pills and salves used by the whites were unknown to the red men, but each of them had in his medicine bag some article, a talisman which he had dreamed about during the drug- and fast-induced hallucinations which were part of his coming-of-age ceremony. This article – it could be a stone, a shell, a feather, or even something with intrinsic value – was always with him, as precious to him as his soul, and its loss was a loss of his manhood.[19]

May places his story within the context of inevitable Indian decline, outlining in his preface the prevailing theory of the Vanishing American:

> Alas, the red race is dying! From the Land of Fire [Tierra del Fuego] to far above the Great Lakes of North America, the smitten giant lies prostrate, struck down by

a pitiless fate, a destiny inexorable . . . It is a cruel law of Nature that the weak must yield to the strong.[20]

But if the Indian is doomed to extinction, the mythology that May created has proved astonishingly long-lived. Not only are his books still in print, with a publishing house, the Karl May Verlag, solely devoted to his works, but every year more than 200,000 people attend the Karl May Festival and Pageant at Bad Segeberg in Holstein, where annually since 1952 live dramatizations of the novels have been performed, together with parades and displays of all kinds, including an Indian Village and a 'Welt der Indianer' (World of Indians) exhibition. Nor is this the only such event. Another festival takes place in Hohenstein-Ernstthal, May's home town in Saxony. Besides performances of theatrical versions of the novels, it also features an Indian Village, which has various activities for adults, children and senior citizens. Visitors can spend a day or even a whole week dressing up as Indians and panning for gold, getting their faces painted, attending lectures on Indian culture, practising archery and horseshoe-throwing, or simply sitting round the camp fire. 'Karl Maynia' has spread to other German-speaking parts of Europe, too, with a Winnetou Festival in the town of Gföhl in Austria. Besides these annual events, there is a regular Karl May magazine (*Karl May & Co.*), which at the time of writing has just published issue no. 98, and a Karl May Institute (Karl May Stiftung) in Radebeul. This is also the site of the Karl May Museum, which claims among other things to display 'the legendary rifles' of Winnetou and Old Shatter-hand and which specializes in material relating to the life and culture of North American Indians. You can purchase from the museum shop a reproduction of May's armchair or a commemorative beer mug.[21]

May also wrote a series of novels set in the Orient, but it is the stories set in the American West that have proved the most durable, and it is May's Indians who have most appealed to the popular German imagination. Generations of young Germans have grown up fantasizing about a life of freedom and adventure, running half-naked through the woods. In May's novels there is virtually no settled society, and none of that opposition between wilderness and the civilization back east that marks many American stories of the West;[22] instead, May's setting is entirely in the untamed lands beyond the frontier, an arcadia or adventure playground where a white man and an Indian can recognize each other's innate nobility and combine forces against the villains. As with that between Natty Bumppo and Chingachgook in Cooper's *The Last of the Mohicans*, it is the relationship between these two that dominates the books.

Germans were not the only Europeans to conceive a passion for Indians. A general fascination with the New World developed across the continent in the later eighteenth century and the nineteenth, fed by writers both American and European, some familiar with their subject matter and others untrammelled in their imagination by mere personal experience. In the course of the nineteenth century fictional production was to be augmented by the appearance of genuine live Indians in Europe. Isolated Indians had travelled to Europe in earlier centuries, including, as previously noted, the celebrated Pocahontas. But the middle of the nineteenth century saw the exhibition of Indians turned into a commercial business, albeit one that was claimed to be conducted for loftier motives than mere profit. In the 1830s George Catlin had travelled west of the Mississippi to paint pictures of the Indian tribes on the Great Plains, who at that time had been little exposed to white civilization. As we have seen, Catlin's avowed intention was to preserve some record of these people before their inevitable demise. Like many Americans at the time, he subscribed to the belief in the Vanishing American, the notion that Indians could not long survive their contact with the whites, a fate he regarded with a melancholy eye:

> Of this sad termination of . . . [the Indians'] existence, there need not be a doubt in the minds of any man who will read the history of their former destruction; contemplating them swept already from two-thirds of the Continent; and who will then travel as I have done, over the vast extent of Frontier, and witness the modes by which the poor fellows are falling, whilst contending for their rights, with acquisitive white men. Such a reader, and such a traveller, I venture to say, if he has not the heart of a brute, will shed tears for them, and be ready to admit that their character and customs, are at this time, a subject of interest and importance, and rendered peculiarly so from the facts that they are

dying at the hands of their Christian neighbours; and, from all experience, that there will probably be no effectual plan instituted, that will save the remainder of them from a similar fate.[23]

Taking their cue from such authorities, European writers were virtually unanimous in seeing Indians as doomed to extinction, and many were not slow to fix blame upon the greed of white American settlers wanting to steal their land, and on the cynical machinations of the federal government, which under the guise of protecting Indians from rapacious whites pushed them off their ancestral territory and marooned them on plots of useless land it called reservations. True, some European authors took a more fatalistic view, preferring to believe that Indians were incapable of adapting and that their fate was therefore sealed: 'As well persuade the eagle to descend from the lofty region in which he exists and live with the fowls of our court-yards, as to prevail upon the red men of North America to become what we call civilized', wrote an English commentator in 1847.[24] The Indians must not be allowed to impede progress, said a writer from eastern Europe in 1858: 'The process of modernization possesses an inalienable right to go ahead and is entitled to push away whatever stands in its way.'[25] A Danish writer argued that the Indian use of land for hunting is uneconomic: 'Such extravagances cannot be afforded in the modern household of the world . . . As they seem to be without a function in the developing economic life, they must be destroyed.'[26] But the majority of European authors were sympathetic to the Indians' plight, if not hopeful about their future. A Russian author stated that 'whites have chased them from their birthplace like animals . . . deceived them in every way; made drunkards of them; armed them against each other, and declared unjust wars against them.'[27] Siding with the Indians against their oppressors led some of the peoples of Europe to identify themselves with the Indians' fate. After the failed insurrection of 1863 against the occupying Russians, the Polish patriot Ludwik Powidaj wrote a celebrated article likening his compatriots to the Indians in their inability to adapt to the facts of modern power politics.[28]

Catlin had no solution to the problem of how to preserve the Indians, but he did have a project designed to keep alive their memory while, so he hoped, making himself some money. He saw his painting as essentially a record that would survive the subjects of his art, so that 'phoenix-like, they may rise from the "stain on a painter's palette." And live again upon the canvass, and stand forth for centuries to come, the living monuments of a noble race.'[29] In 1841 Catlin took his pictures on a tour of Britain, attracting more than 30,000 visitors at a shilling per head.[30] From the start he clearly had an urge to dramatize the representations in his pictures, to go beyond what mere paint and canvas could do. To illustrate the lectures that accompanied viewings of his pictures, Catlin would dress himself up as an Indian chief, with 'deer-skin habiliments, profusely ornamented with scalp-locks, beads, porcupine quill, and various other decorations'.[31] He would

George Catlin's sketch of his exhibition in the Louvre in Paris, 1845.

demonstrate the use of Indian weapons and perform Indian dances. He even went to society balls in Indian dress. Later he hired actors to present tableaux vivants, with English men playing warriors and boys playing Indian women. He alternated two programmes, one based on warfare, one on domestic life; not surprisingly, the former, with scenes of a war-dance, an ambush and scalping, proved more popular with audiences.[32] All this seemed to lead inexorably towards the full-scale presentation of the authentic article, and in 1843 Catlin added some real live Indians (a group of Ojibwas) to his exhibition and accompanied them to Windsor Castle, where they performed dances in front of Queen Victoria. Subsequently Catlin employed another group of Indians, Iowas this time, to exhibit themselves at Lord's cricket ground.[33] Though the Indians demonstrated Indian games such as lacrosse and played musical instruments, the chief selling-point was again the scenes of warfare, Catlin pointing out to his audiences that real scalps were used in the war-dances.[34]

Not all those who saw them were equally enthusiastic. Charles Dickens was cruelly disillusioned, making mock of any pretension that audiences were witnessing the noble savage:

> Mr Catlin was an energetic earnest man, who had lived among more tribes of Indians than I need reckon up here, and had written a picturesque and glowing book about them. With his party of Indians squatting and spitting on the table before him, or dancing their miserable jigs after their own dreary manner, he called, in all good faith, upon his civilised audience to take notice of their symmetry and grace, their perfect limbs, and the exquisite expression of their pantomime; and his civilised audience, in all good faith, complied and admired. Whereas, as mere animals, they were wretched creatures, very low in the scale and very poorly formed; and as men and women possessing any power of truthful dramatic expression by means of action, they were no better than the chorus at an Italian Opera in England.[35]

But Dickens was the exception. In general Europeans responded enthusiastically to Catlin's presentation of Indians, praising their dignity and comeliness. In 1845 Catlin paraded the troupe of Iowas in front of Louis-Philippe, King of the French, and his paintings were viewed by the élite of Parisian artistic society, including Charles Baudelaire, George Sand and Eugène Delacroix.[36]

Later in the century came the full-scale commodification of the Wild West in the form of Buffalo Bill Cody's travelling show, which turned the exhibition of the West into a highly profitable business. Indians formed an integral part of Cody's spectacle. His first trip to Europe took place in 1887; one visitor, Queen Victoria, was particularly impressed and wrote up the experience in her diary:

> All the different people, wild, painted Red Indians from America, on their wild bare backed horses, of different tribes – cow boys [sic], Mexicans, etc., all came tearing round at full speed, shrieking & screaming, which had the weirdest effect. An attack on a coach & on a ranch, with an immense amount of firing, was most exciting, so was the buffalo hunt, & the bucking ponies, that were almost impossible to sit. The cow boys are fine looking people, but the painted Indians, with their feathers & wild dress (very little of it) were rather alarming looking, & they have cruel faces.[37]

It was Cody who was responsible in large measure for fixing a certain image of the Indian in the popular European mind. His success in Europe was immense; in a series of tours his company covered the major countries of Western Europe, including Britain, France, Spain, Italy and Germany, as well as Austria and Hungary. Other Wild West shows, such as Doc Carver's 'Wild America', complete with Indians, toured eastern Europe in the 1890s, visiting Budapest, Warsaw, St Petersburg, Helsinki and Stockholm. As a result there was an immense outpouring of cheap fiction on Western topics, including European imitations of the dime novels based on Buffalo Bill and other heroes, such as the German *Buffalo Bill die Sioux-schlacht am Grabstein*.[38]

In *Dubliners* (1914) James Joyce recounted the effects of such publications on children's games:

Buffalo Bill (seated) in Venice *c.* 1890, with Indian performers who include Long Bear and American Horse (in feather head-dresses).

It was Joe Dillon who introduced the Wild West to us. He had a little library made up of old numbers of the *Union Jack*, *Pluck* and *The Halfpenny Marvel*. Every evening after school we met in his back garden and arranged Indian battles. He and his fat young brother Leo the idler held the loft of the stable while we tried to carry it by storm . . . He looked like some kind of Indian when he capered round the garden, an old tea-cosy on his head, beating a tin with his fist and yelling 'Ya! Yaka, yaka, yaka!'[39]

When the cinema arrived at the end of the nineteenth century, it was only the latest in a plethora of commercial entertainments that drew upon a certain idea of the Indian to excite the popular imagination. Not only did Europeans consume American film Westerns in large numbers; soon they were making their own. As early as 1903 there was a British film version of Longfellow's *Hiawatha*, made for the Urban company. Many of the thirty or so Westerns made in Britain before 1915 had Indian themes, as for example the Hepworth company's *The Squatter's Daughter* (1906), one of the very few of such films to survive. Luke McKernan describes it:

Rumoured to have been shot on Putney Common, London, the action opens with Indians crawling through undergrowth towards a ranch house. They beat down the fence and spear the men inside, taking a girl captive. She is taken to the chief, who declines to kill her with his spear, and instead she is tied to a stake to be burnt. Her father, riding past, hears the commotion, shoots down the Indians and rescues his daughter from the stake.[40]

The capture and rescue plot follows directly from the novels of Fenimore Cooper, from a myriad dime novels and from the narrative elements of Buffalo Bill's show. A less lurid, more wistfully romantic view of Indians emerges in Jean Durand's film *Coeur ardent* (1912), a Western shot in the south of France, in the Camargue, a wild region that passes for the American prairies. A young Indian seeks to marry a chief's daughter, but lacks the requisite bride price. When he is captured by enemies from another tribe, she helps him escape. The film has a real feel for the beauties of landscape and, like some American Westerns of the period, the story takes place entirely within Indian society, in an idealized world before conflict with whites. The film stars Joë Hamman, a French enthusiast of all things Western who had visited America and met Buffalo Bill. Durand and Hamman were to make several Westerns together in the period before the First World War.

Most of the nations of Europe have had a go at making Westerns at some stage. But for the most part the early attempts did not get beyond tales of exciting escapism. The American West was treated as essentially no different from any other sphere of adventure such as Africa or the Far East. It was not until the 1960s that Europeans seized on the West as a subject offering more substantial themes. The Italian Westerns of the 1960s, the best-known European efforts in the genre, scarcely ever involve Indians. Sergio Leone apparently 'hated Indian scenes' in Westerns, although it's not clear why.[41] When it wanted to mount a critique of Yankee imperialism, the spaghetti Western preferred to use Mexicans. But in Germany, with its long-standing fascination with the Indian, fuelled by the fictions of Karl May and others, things were different.

Given the huge readership of May's novels, it is surprising that it was not until the 1960s, at a time when, paradoxically, the American Western was going into a long-term decline, that they were first made into films. When it appeared in 1962 *Der Schatz im Silbersee* was the most expensive film yet made in West Germany, and subsequently proved to be the most successful, being exported to sixty countries. It initiated a cycle of eleven Westerns based on May's books between 1962 and 1968. Cast as Winnetou was the former French paratrooper Pierre Brice, playing opposite Hollywood's Tarzan, Lex Barker, as Shatterhand, or Stewart Granger as Old Surehand. Shot in the mountains of northern Yugoslavia, the films are a good approximation to the ethos of May's novels, as Old Shatterhand, the blonde white man, and his blood-brother Winnetou, the noble savage, forge the bonds of friendship in their joint struggle against bad men.

As the extent of the cycle of films would suggest, they were enormously popular. The theme tune of the first film, 'Old Shatterhand Melodie', topped the West German singles chart for seventeen weeks. 'Soon there were board and card games, hundreds of toys, countless comics, coffee-table and drawing-books, even a cookbook, whole clothes ranges including socks, towels, glasses, shoes and a brand of cigarettes based on film motifs and characters.'[42]

As Tassilo Schneider remarks, whereas the Italian Westerns of Leone and his epigones attempted a deconstruction of the genre, undermining its ideology of the civilizing mission of the noble and dedicated hero, in the vanguard of the advancing white settlers, the Karl May films aimed at a reconstruction, a reversion to an earlier, more innocent age of cinema in which virtue is unquestioned and villainy is defeated. Often the films begin with a voice-over enunciating the mission of the Apache chief Winnetou, which is to bring about peace and reconciliation between the Indians and the whites. In *Winnetou I* (1963) we are informed that Winnetou's tribe, the Mescalero Apache, were originally friendly to the whites, but have been forced into hostility because the whites lusted after the gold on Apache lands; and now the railroad is threatening to intrude upon their territory. Old Shatterhand endeavours to persuade the company to go around the Apache homeland, but the rapacious Santer and his gang of white renegades are intent on provoking war in order to gain access to the Apaches' gold.

The plots are formulaic but complicated, with characters endlessly captured, then rescued, then captured again. There's always some broad humour, often featuring comic old-timer Sam Hawkens (a May invention), and there's a pretty girl, usually assigned to a young suitor, not to the heroes. The motivation of the plot is the whites' lust for gold or some other kind of wealth, invariably seen as a source of

Marie Versini as Nscho-tschi and Pierre Brice as Winnetou in Harald Reinl's *Winnetou I* (1963).

evil. The Indians live in a pre-industrial society, a state of innocence in which they have no need of money. Winnetou, with shoulder-length black hair and disconcertingly blue eyes, is a figure of uncomplicated virtue and selflessness, devoting himself like a medieval knight to the righting of wrongs and the rescuing of maidens in distress. In each film he wears the same pristine costume, a suit of fringed white buckskin decorated with blue and white beading, and carries a long rifle decorated with silver studs. Winnetou and Old Shatterhand begin as enemies in *Winnetou I*; they fight and Old Shatterhand is wounded. At the Apache camp, an impressive if surprising structure of multi-storeyed buildings, like that of Taos Pueblo in New Mexico, Shatterhand is nursed back to health by Winnetou's sister, Nscho-tschi, who is dressed almost identically to her brother, in white buckskin, decorated with bead-work. (Ethnographic accuracy is not a strong point in the films; the Indian camps, for example, whether identified as

Ute, Shoshone, Comanche or whatever, although picturesquely presented, with lots of drumming and dancing, almost invariably feature a totem pole or two, actually an artefact confined to the Indians of the north-west.)

After Shatterhand and Winnetou have been reconciled, Nscho-tschi agrees to go to school so that she can learn the white man's ways and thus she and Shatterhand may be married. But, predictably, before the end of the film she is shot by the evil Santer. Winnetou and Old Shatterhand affirm the primacy of their relationship by becoming blood-brothers, cutting their arms in order to mingle bodily fluids. In *Winnetou II* (1964) the Apache chief appears to be loosening this bond when he falls in love with a young woman from the Assiniboine tribe, Ribanna. A gang of whites led by Forrester (Anthony Steele) is trying to provoke hostilities with the Ponca Indians, and in response many tribes are gathering for a war, with the Colonel of the local fort convinced the Indians

Pierre Brice as Winnetou and Lex Barker as Old Shatterhand in Harald Reinl's *Winnetou II* (1964).

need to be taught a lesson. But the Colonel's son proposes a radical plan to bring about peace, a marriage between himself and the beautiful Ribanna. Winnetou, in a spirit of noble self-sacrifice, renounces his claim to her, and after he and Old Shatterhand have defeated the bad men peace is proclaimed. Winnetou and Old Shatterhand ride away together into the pristine mountains of northern Yugoslavia. Such landscapes are the perfect setting for the idyllic world that Winnetou inhabits, with clear, blue lakes into which tumble picturesque waterfalls. They correspond closely to the paintings of the Rocky Mountains produced in the 1860s by the German-born and Düsseldorf-trained artist Albert Bierstadt and which was for a time, until the taste for deserts and canyons replaced it, the paradigm of what the west of America should look like. When on occasion the German filmmakers import a cactus into the location to suggest the more arid landscape of the Southwest, the effect is jarring.

Interestingly, whereas in May's novels the Germanic characteristics of Old Shatterhand are insisted on, in Lex Barker's interpretation he is indistinguishable from an American hero. Undoubtedly this helped the success of the films in foreign markets. As a result the Karl May phenomenon, as refracted through the movie versions, was eventually to become relatively well-known in the English-speaking world (even though Christopher Frayling, discussing May in the context of the Italian Western, which the West German Westerns helped usher on to the stage, noted that at the time of writing (1981) not one of May's novels had appeared in English).[43]

What remains less well known, because it had no equivalent international distribution, is the cycle of Westerns produced in East Germany by DEFA, the state film company. Released between 1966 and 1985, there was a total of fourteen *Indianerfilme*, as they were known, some of them based, if loosely, on Fenimore Cooper's novels. Though primarily intended as escapist fare (and among the most successful films the company produced), they come, inevitably, with an unmistakable political message. Whereas the West German films are content to enact May's adventure fantasies in a never-never land, the East German films attempt to tie in their plots to a particular set of social and economic circumstances. Thus in *Apachen* (*Apaches*, 1973), a campaign by the Apache warrior Ulzana is set at a time just before the Mexican–American War that began in 1846. (The real Ulzana, otherwise known as Josanie, led a celebrated raid in New Mexico in 1885.) A group of white Americans come over the border into Mexico and massacre a band of Apaches in order to collect the bounty on their scalps. The underlying motive is that the American authorities have their eyes on the local copper mine and wish to clear the Apaches from the region before they invade. Thus the Apaches are seen to stand directly in the way of aggressively expansionist American capitalism. Ulzana leads the remnants of his band in a series of revenge attacks against the American miners and the Mexicans who assisted in the massacre, attacks notable for their boldness and bravery.

In *Chingachgook, die grosse Schlage* (*Chingachgook the Great Snake*, 1967), loosely based on Fenimore Cooper's *The*

Deerslayer and set in 1740, the political lesson is set out clearly at the start. The colonial powers, Britain and France, exploit the Indians by buying their furs cheap and selling them goods at high prices. Later, a British officer (effete and arrogant) explains to a subordinate that 'we must decimate the Indians'. Let them exterminate each other, he argues. 'The crown wants power and riches.' There appears to be a contradiction here. If the Indians are exterminated, how can Britain continue to exploit them? But the strategy of setting Indian tribes against each other is working in favour of the British. The Delawares and the Hurons have a long-standing feud, which leads to the capture of Chingachgook's bride-to-be. Eventually Chingachgook brokers a peace between the tribes with the assistance of his friend the Deerslayer, a buckskin-clad blond man who sides with the Indians. The Deerslayer delivers his own pro-Indian messages, arguing, for example, that

Gojko Mitic (at back of canoe) with Rolf Römer in Richard Groschopp's *Chingachgook the Great Snake* (1967).

Gojko Mitic in Gottfried Kolditz's *Apache* (1973).

although the whites did not invent the practice of scalping, it is they who have made it into a paying business (this being, in the East German Marxist view, one of the worst accusations one can make against a practice).

All the whites, with the exception of the Deerslayer and Judith, a girl he falls for but will not marry because she wishes to leave the woods and return to civilization, are presented as cruel and corrupt. By contrast, both Delawares and Hurons are essentially peace-loving, despite their feud. In his novels such as *The Last of the Mohicans* Cooper makes a distinction between the Hurons, almost unremittingly evil, and the noble Chingachgook and his son Uncas, the last of their tribe, the Mohicans. But for the DEFA studios, Indians are always good. It is the whites, whether Yankees or British, who are the instigators of evil. In *Chingachgook the Great*

Snake one of the whites, Harry, even comes out with the most clichéd of all racist remarks, that the only good Indian is a dead Indian (a remark historically attributed to the Civil War general Phil Sheridan).

Just as the West German Karl May adaptations had used a foreign actor for the chief Indian role, presumably in order to signify an ethnic difference, so the East German productions also cast a non-German. Appearing as the leading Indian character in twelve of the *Indianerfilme* was Gojko Mitic, a Yugoslav who had worked as a bit player and stunt man before being plunged into a starring role in *Die Söhne der grossen Bärin* (*The Sons of the Great Bear*, 1966). Mitic's dark good looks, with high cheekbones, made him a star in East Germany, though his accented German meant that in the films he was always dubbed. After the fall of the Berlin Wall Mitic came west and took over from Pierre Brice the role of Winnetou in the open-air dramatizations of Karl May novels at Bad Sege- berg, also playing Winnetou in some television adaptations of Karl May novels. For the DEFA studios' *Indianerfilme* he played several historical Indian characters, including Tecumseh, the great leader of the Shawnees, Ulzana (in a film of that name set in the 1880s and based on the historical facts) and Osceola, the chief of the Seminoles during the war of 1835–43. This latter film, shot in Cuba, which effectively doubles as Florida, naturally takes the Indians' side against the slave-owning whites. The Indians show solidarity, in the spirit of the Communist Internationale, with escaped black slaves. At one point there is an interesting discussion between two of the white slave-owners on the question of modernization. One argues that slaves are the best way of harvesting the sugar cane on which their profits depend. But another, arguing a classic Marxist position, shows off his new mechanized cane-mill and explains that mechanization is the way forward, and that slavery is not only immoral but inefficient.

In *Blutsbrüder* (*Blood Brothers*, 1975) Mitic plays Harter Felsen, an Indian who becomes the blood brother of Harmonica, an American soldier who deserts after a massacre of an Indian village by the army. Harmonica is played by Dean Reed, an American singer who became a Communist and emigrated to the GDR. Harmonica falls in love with Harter Felsen's sister Rehkitz, but, as in *Winnetou* and *Broken Arrow*, the fantasy of interracial marriage is snuffed out before it can take hold. One critic has described Mitic's work as particularly suited to the ethos of official East German cinema:

Gojko Mitic with Gisela Freudenberg in Werner Wallroth's *Blood Brothers* (1975).

Director Konrad Petzold praised Mitic as a professional and an ideological role model. 'It is not as if Gojko had no other choice than to portray Indians here in the East. He had, and as far as I know he continues to have, offers from the capitalist countries. It's a sign of his straightforwardness and honesty that he chooses to work here exclusively. He is really serious about this work, and it is important to him to participate in the new discoveries and the new developments of this genre, according to our Marxist view of history.' Mitic's offscreen characteristics, which biographer Ehrentraud Novotny describes as 'understated, disciplined, modest, hard-working, reliable, sympathetic and companionable,' combined with his onscreen courage, athleticism and good looks, wisdom and leadership; just as the athlete Gojko Mitic is a convinced anti-alcoholic, his Indians will not be fooled by 'firewater' either. These qualities make him a role model for children, the dream of teenage girls, and an ideal son-in-law, a particularly Teutonic form of model Indian and model citizen. One commentator described the reaction of fans: 'When Gojko was on the scene, we had mass rallies that weren't even ordered from above.'[44]

Certainly, when I met him at a festival of European Westerns in Udine in Italy in 1997, Mitic was happy to talk about his work, unfailingly polite and modest. While not taking himself over-seriously, he had no inclination to send up the films or adopt a camp attitude. He seemed sincere in his work.

Recent commentators have tried to dig deeper into why Indians should have such a widespread and lasting appeal to German-speaking people. On the face of it, it does seem strange that every year some two or three thousand people attend the annual meeting of the Westernbund, an association of Indian hobbyist clubs for people who want to practise the Indian way of life. At such meetings they engage in singing and dancing to Indian music, story-telling and handicrafts, while camping out in tipis. The Westernbund is an association of more than 120 clubs originally formed in the Federal Republic of Germany, although it includes clubs from Belgium, Switzerland and France. There is a corresponding organization, the Indianistikbund, for clubs originating in the former German Democratic Republic: over a thousand people attended their annual get-together in 2002, erecting 399 tipis on the site. Whereas the Westernbund includes people whose interests are in cowboys or in the Civil War, the Indianistikbund, as its name suggest, is preoccupied solely with Indians.

The appeal of camping out in the open air is obvious enough. The question is, why with these groups does it take the form of imitating the lifestyle of people with whom contemporary Germans seem to have so little in common? Historically, it has been suggested, the nineteenth century saw the formation of a mythical origin for the German peoples by grafting the image of forest-dwelling Teutonic tribes (described by Tacitus in *De origine et situ Germanorum* as prototypes of the noble savage, brave, loyal and fierce in battle against the Romans) onto the legend of Siegfried, the tragic hero betrayed by back-stabbers, the originals of those who were to 'betray' the nation at various points in the twentieth century. In this myth the Indians become honorary Teutons who, like the Germans, have been the victims of history. Impersonating Indians, it has been argued, allows the Germans to 'refuse the role of perpetrator in racial aggression. Indian impersonation thus facilitated the work of restitution, by allowing Germans to explore alternative [to Nazi] notions of ethnic differences and to reject learned concepts of Aryan supremacy.'[45] In this process, the DEFA films can make a special contribution: 'Refusing to be a powerless victim of a genocide, Mitic acts out the fantasy of the resistance fighter and antifascist, providing a role model for young citizens and relieving older ones from responsibilities they may not have been up to during the rise of Nazism and Hitler's rule.'[46] At the same time it allows Germans to identify with fellow victims of foreign invasion (most of the clubs were formed soon after the Second World War), and in the East enthusiasm for Indians received special approval in that it coincided with official doctrines about the aggressiveness of the United States and the need for solidarity with the Third World.

However, this may not be the whole story. Other motivations have been alleged. Some of the enthusiasm undoubtedly derives from a belief that Indians are more ecologically minded, and in a country such as Germany where 'Greens' have a strong position this gives Indians a powerful appeal. Indian life can be portrayed, moreover, as an alterative to consumer capitalism, offering instead a simpler life based more on communal values. For example, it is usual in the Indianistikbund get-togethers for the preparation of meals to be part of a collective process. In addition, a student of the phenomenon suggests:

> To most hobbyists Indians embody an intact social order in harmony with nature – an essentially antimodern fantasy. Yolanda Broyles-González's study of the 'Black Forest Cheyenne,' a hobbyist club in southern Germany, argues that Indian impersonation allowed club members to express fear of modernization, grief over geographical and social displacement, and mourning of lost indigenous traditions, but also to validate and celebrate a past marked by rural artisan lifeways and a primarily oral culture.[47]

Such explanations may seem both too far-fetched for such relatively inconsequential behaviour, and at the same time too obvious. Must everything in German behaviour be explained in relation to its recent history? In any case, two or three thousand people represent only a tiny minority of the population: is the phenomenon so significant? Nor should we ignore the fact that Germans themselves are able to laugh at such behaviour. In contrast to the po-faced sincerity of both the West and East German Indian films of the 1960s, one of the most popular German productions of recent years is *Der Schuh des Manitu* (2001), a send-up of those earlier films, in which Abahachi, a chief of the Apache Indians, and his white blood-brother Ranger have a series of comic adventures, together with Winnetouch, Abahachi's twin brother, who is gay. Much of the film's humour relies on the audience being familiar with the films of the 1960s that it parodies.

By the early 1970s France had developed a highly politicized film culture in the wake of the social upheavals consequent upon the *événements* of 1968. One curious effect was a sudden outbreak of films best described as 'counter-Westerns'. Whereas the West German films had been offered as pure entertainment, whatever their hidden ideological messages, and those of East Germany had been intended to reflect the official doctrines of the state, whatever the use that audiences actually made of them, the French Westerns were intentionally oppositional, seeking to make a direct political comment both upon American cinema and the established bourgeois society of the west that created it. Jean-Luc Godard's *Vent d'est* (1970), Luc Moullet's *Une Aventure de Billy the Kid* (1971) and Jacques Brel's *Far West* (1973) are only marginally if at all concerned with Indians. But Marco Ferreri's *Touche pas la femme blanche* (1973) is a full-scale reconstruction of the Battle of the Little Big Horn, set in modern-day Paris with the climactic scenes shot on a huge building site. Marcello Mastroianni plays a vainglorious Custer, with Michel Piccoli as a boastful and cowardly Buffalo Bill Cody and Alain Cluny as Sitting Bull ('Taureau Assis'). The attack upon the Indians is engineered for their own ends by a group of politicians and businessmen. Custer is recruited because he will do anything for glory, and Buffalo Bill is

Alain Cluny as
Taureau Assis
(Sitting Bull) in
Marco Ferreri's
*Touche pas la
femme blanche*
(1973).

brought in because a war against the Indians might be unpop-
ular and it needs his showbiz expertise to sell it. These historical figures prove equally pompous and self-serving; at one
point Custer is in a bookshop signing copies of his autobiography when Cody bursts in and begins reading excerpts from
his own. The humour is as broad as the political message is
stark; overall the film plays like a poor man's version of a
Brecht play, with the Indians grist in the mill of the filmmakers'
political agenda.

The French fascination with the American west, and
with Indians in particular, continues to show itself in the
scores of comic books published, as for example in the *Blue-
berry* series by Jean-Michel Charlier and Jean Giraud, turned
into a film in 2004.[48] It's no surprise that when Disneyland
established itself in Paris, it should feature as one of its main
attractions a re-enactment of Buffalo Bill's Wild West,

complete with Indians, whom you may hear singing on the company's website.[49] More than a hundred years after the cinema first brought moving images of Indians to Europe, they still have the power to kindle the imagination.

5 indians not injuns

The Indian of Hollywood, the mounted, befeathered warrior with his tomahawk or war-bow, is predominantly the Indian of the Plains. Sioux, Cheyenne, Comanche: these are the Indians against whom the advancing whites fought a series of battles in the post-Civil War period, while in the south-west the US army struggled to contain the Apache, only finally succeeding with the surrender of Geronimo in 1886. But at the end of the nineteenth century another kind of Indian came to prominence, one whose appeal lay not in his capacity for stirring action and threatening violence, but in its opposite.

The Pueblo Indians were first encountered by whites in the mid-sixteenth century. Coronado's expedition, journeying north from Mexico into what is now Arizona and New Mexico, discovered a series of Indian villages whose inhabitants lived in permanent structures of stone and adobe, often multi-storeyed, and practised agriculture by raising corn, beans and squash in locations such as Zuni, Acoma and Taos. Though speaking separate languages, these people shared many aspects of their culture.

Despite a series of revolts, the Spanish were able to impose themselves militarily. What they failed to do to any great extent was to extirpate the Indians' culture, and above all their religion. Some Pueblo peoples, such as the Hopi, have resisted Christianity to this day, and the Pueblo settlements have displayed remarkable durability in centuries of radical change for Indian peoples.

The Spanish regarded many Pueblo practices, such as the Hopi snake dance, in which men performed ritual acts with rattlesnakes, as disgusting and barbaric. But by the end of the nineteenth century the new science of anthropology was beginning to take a different view. Franz Boas was at the forefront of these developments in his study of the Indians of the north-west, which led him to the belief that, contrary to earlier views, Indian society was not best understood as a primitive stage in the evolution of civilization, one from which Indians might eventually graduate to a higher level along the route taken by Europeans. Instead, the idea emerged that Indian societies, diverse in themselves, might represent different models for culture. In 1882 Boas wrote:

> I often ask myself what advantages our 'good society' possesses over that of the 'savages'. The more I see of their customs, the more I realize that we have no right to look down on them. Where amongst our people would you find such true hospitality? . . . We have no right to blame them for their forms and superstitions which may seem ridiculous to us. We 'highly educated people' are much worse, relatively speaking.[1]

Frank Cushing, a trained ethnologist from the Bureau of American Ethnology, went to Zuni Pueblo in New Mexico in 1879 for a field trip intended to last two months. He ended up staying four years, during which time he became fluent in the Zuni language, became a member of the tribal council and was initiated into the priesthood. His writings provided a comprehensive insight into another culture with its own values, different but not inferior. Cushing even seems to have come to believe that in some sense he really was an Indian, recording that a voice told him that 'you are the soul of an Indian of olden times'.[2] He was not the last white to seek to merge his identity into Indian culture.

If advances in ethnography underpinned a change in attitudes towards Indian societies, it was a combination of other forces, some of them high-minded, some much less disinterested, which was responsible for bringing the Pueblo peoples to the notice of mainstream America. In 1898 the artist Ernest Blumenschein came by accident to Taos in New Mexico, the most northerly of the Pueblos. He later described his first impressions after an arduous journey through the mountains: 'It had to end in the Taos valley, green with trees and fields of alfalfa, populated by dark-skinned people who greeted me pleasantly. Then I saw my first Taos Indian, blankets artistically draped. New Mexico had gripped me.'[3] Together with fellow artists, including Bert Phillips, Joseph Henry Sharp, Oscar Berninghaus and Eanger Irving Couse, Blumenschein eventually took up residence in Taos, and the group was to formalize itself in 1915 as the Taos Society of

Bert Geer Phillips, *Song of the Aspen*, c. 1926, oil on canvas.

Artists. Its members committed themselves both to the encouragement of art locally and to the preservation of indigenous cultures. Though several of these artists were seduced by the beauties of the south-western landscape, much of their work focused on Indians. As a catalogue to an exhibition of pictures by Berninghaus remarked, 'in much of our Western

Joseph Henry Sharp (1859–1953), *Father and Son*, oil on canvas.

landscape we need the Indian in the same way that a finely wrought piece of gold needs a jewel to set off its beauty in a piece of jewelry.'[4]

This might suggest that the interest in Indians did not extend beyond their capacity to provide local colour. But it went a great deal deeper than that. In place of the increasing materialism of white culture, the Pueblos offered a model of a society in which everything was touched by spiritual values, in which religion was not separate but suffused every aspect of life. Instead of the heartless mechanization of industrial production, the Indians practised artisanal crafts, with pottery, weaving and basketwork done by hand. Instead of a society devoted to breakneck progress with the devil take the hindmost, Pueblo society offered a model of stability, a non-competitive society in which everyone had a secure place. In formulating this vision of Indian life, the artists undoubtedly closed their eyes to much of what stared them in the face: the ravages of white society upon Indians, poverty, lack of educational provision, alcoholism and other forms of social breakdown. Instead they chose to accentuate the positive and portray Indians as dignified and aesthetically pleasing. Accordingly, as Richard Frost has written:

> Starting about 1890 and growing rapidly after 1910, a new attitude emerged. By the 1920s, in the popular mind the Pueblos were the most interesting of the American Indian tribes. Their positive qualities had grown larger than life. They were admired as ceremonialists and artists. Their pottery was sought by discriminating connoisseurs and curio-hunters. The beauty of their villages was interpreted in oil paintings displayed in prestigious eastern art galleries. Books and magazines sympathetically portrayed Pueblo life, and the style of their architecture inspired the remodelling of the capital city of New Mexico. The Pueblo Indian romance, a generation in the making, was fully ripe.[5]

The Taos artists were influenced by modernism's fascination with the 'primitive', and also by the desire for a truly indigenous art, not one in debt to European models. In the Indians the artists found 'the oldest of American civilisations. The manners and customs and style of architecture are the same today that they were before Christ was born. They offer the painter a subject as full of the fundamental qualities of life as did the Holy Land of long ago.'[6] Indians, then, could provide the prestige of an old civilization that American society felt it lacked, and one which offered an alternative to and refuge from the ills of modern life.

Writers as well as artists flocked to Taos. Among those who made extended visits after 1915 were Willa Cather, Robert Frost, Thornton Wilder, John Galsworthy and Sinclair Lewis. D. H. Lawrence lived on a ranch outside Taos for eighteen months in 1924–5. He wrote about the Indians in his usual apocalyptic fashion:

> The Indians keep burning an eternal fire, the sacred fire of the old dark religion. To the vast white America, either in our generation or in the time of our children, will come some fearful convulsion. Some terrible convulsion will take place among the millions of this country, sooner or later. When the pueblos are gone. But oh, let us have the grace and dignity to shelter these ancient centres of life, so that, if die they must, they die a natural death. And at the same time, let us try to adjust ourselves again to the Indian outlook, to take up an old dark thread from their vision, and see again as they see, without forgetting we are ourselves.[7]

Both Indian art itself (blankets, pottery, jewellery, baskets, sand-paintings) and the representations of Indian life made by the Taos artists offered a perspective on indigenous cultures quite different from the views of plains Indians that the popular media provided in the second half of the nineteenth century. Instead of a warlike people hostile to the whites, Pueblo Indians could be represented as peaceable and domesticated. Artists such as Couse and Sharp showed Indians engaged in creative pursuits: playing musical instruments, dancing, preparing food and decorating pottery. Such views did not attract Frederic Remington, the artist who had the most influence on the image of the Indians upon which popular forms such as dime novels, Wild West shows, stage plays and, eventually, the cinema were to draw so heavily. They were 'too tame', he wrote. 'They don't appeal to me – too decorative – and too easily in reach of every tenderfoot.'[8] What Remington wanted was action, not the repose and calmness that the Taos artists found in Indian life.

Remington tried to help Bert Phillips sell his paintings in New York, but declared that he could not find a market.[9] Yet by the turn of the century the commercial possibilities of Taos art had been energetically developed by one of the most modern and dynamic forces in contemporary society, the railroads. In 1878 the Atchison, Topeka and Santa Fe Railroad (ATSF) signed a contract with the restaurateur Fred Harvey, which led to a chain of station lunchrooms, hotels and dining cars along its tracks. Under its ambitious advertising manager William Haskell Simpson, the ATSF, in association with the

Harvey Company, used the artistic production of the south-west to promote its services.

Beginning in 1907, the Santa Fe produced an annual calendar that showcased the paintings of Taos artists. Couse was particularly favoured. The Indians in his pictures, grouped picturesquely round campfires engaged in such tasks as painting pottery or making turquoise beads, are sedentary, productively engaged and non-threatening. The railroad had its own ideas about what Indians ought to look like, preferring them to appear noble and dignified, and Simpson was not above giving advice, as when he wrote to Couse: 'The figure of the Chief doesn't look quite tall enough for one entitled to that name. Perhaps the "squattiness" may be due to the war bonnet being so wide, or possibly to the way the blanket hangs. No doubt you can overcome this when working from the model.'[10]

In 1901 the Harvey Company formed an Indian Department, based in Albuquerque, New Mexico, the purpose of which was both to collect Indian artefacts, exhibiting them as an amenity to its customers, and to market Indian goods to tourists in search of souvenirs. Indian craftsmen and crafts-women were employed to work on the premises of Harvey hotels, where they might produce articles for sale and at the same time function as an exotic and colourful spectacle for travellers. Harvey also exploited the increasing popularity of the postcard, producing literally thousands of different examples, of which Indian subjects formed a substantial proportion.

In the manner of the Taos artists, the postcards empha-sized the domesticated Indian over the warlike variety favoured

Saleroom in the Fred Harvey Indian Building hotel in Albuquerque, New Mexico, c. 1905.

Navajo weavers at the Fred Harvey Indian Building hotel, c. 1905.

Adam Clark Vroman, *Navajo Silversmith*, 1901.

by Remington and his epigones. They were often based on hand-coloured photographs by a group of photographers who specialized in images of the Pueblo Indians. Named the Pasadena Eight, they included Carl Moon, Adam Clark Vroman (whose bookstore is still trading on East Colorado Boulevard, Pasadena), George Wharton James, Frederick Monsen and Charles Lummis, an enthusiastic promoter of the south-west in books such as *The Land of Poco Tiempo* (1893) and the founder of *Out West* magazine. It was Lummis who coined the phrase 'See America First', an admonition to travellers among his fellow countrymen that was the tourist equivalent of the artistic nationalism of the Taos Society.

Monsen wrote that:

> Only to be among these Indians, to hear them talk, and to observe their treatment of one another, and of the casual stranger that is within their gates, is to have forced upon one the realization that here is the unspoiled remnant of a great race, a race of men who have, from time immemorial, lived quiet, sane, wholesome lives very close to nature.[11]

Harvey commissioned postcards from the Detroit Photographic Company very much in this spirit, idealizing Indian life in a very different manner from that of the Buffalo Bill and Remington tradition. The intention was to market the south-west as a region of exotic and picturesque charm (a process that continued with the addition to New Mexico car licence plates of the phrase 'Land of Enchantment' in 1941). As a historian of the Detroit Photographic Company records:

> At a time when the Southwest remained one of the few regions tourists still insisted they'd rather travel through at night than during the daytime, Harvey's decision to use the Detroit Photographic Company and the postcard medium as a means of generating a new and more positive image, was brilliant . . . Harvey's sets resurrected the Indian first by focusing on the gentle exotica of the Pueblo tribes – by showing their 'thrilling' snake dances and homing in on their everyday lives . . .

Navajo medicine men, an 'Apache War Party,' Indians on horseback, Indians in ceremonial garb, Indians in all possible poses designed to suggest to the viewer the possibility of re-enacting a mythological Western past without danger to self or property.[12]

Whereas the Remington tradition preferred its Indians as bloodthirsty as possible, any references to 'war parties' in Harvey pictures were carefully sanitized by being placed firmly in the past. A Harvey postcard titled 'In Apache Land' shows two tipis and the caption reads:

The Apache Indians were until recently the most warlike of all the Southwestern Indians and have caused the government of the United States, as well as the early settlers, no end of trouble. Today, with their numbers fast diminishing, and with several forts on or near their scattered reservations, with the railroad as an ally the government has no trouble with them and the Indian has turned his talents to the weaving of baskets and plaques and is at last enjoying the fruits of his labours in peace.[13]

The assertion that the Indian is diminishing in numbers, that he is 'vanishing', and that the threat posed by Geronimo has been eradicated through the conversion of the Indian towards peaceful occupations, is intended to reassure the timid tourist. A name that once sent fear through the white

'Baking Bread, Pueblo of Tesuque, New Mexico', in a Fred Harvey postcard.

community was now sufficiently anodyne for the Santa Fe to name one of its trains 'Geronimo'. Besides postcards, the Harvey Company and the ATSF made extensive use of lectures, accompanied by slides of Indians, which were performed in educational establishments and on the trains themselves. The burden of the talks echoed the other forms of publicity, emphasizing the picturesqueness of the Indians, with slides of

Hopi dances, or of Indians engaged in a variety of crafts. The extent to which the postcards feminize Indian life is notable, too. There is barely a single woman to be seen in the entire artistic output of Frederic Remington. For him Indians are masculine, fierce and warlike. But the Harvey postcards show women engaged in the production of pots or blankets, making bread, doing their hair and minding children. Even the men

'Navajo woman and papoose, New Mexico', a Fred Harvey postcard.

are often busy at tasks, such as weaving, that are associated with a sedentary, domesticated life.

In 1905 the Harvey Company opened the Hopi House, built on its facilities at the Grand Canyon (the railroad had reached the Canyon in 1901). Designed in the Indian style, the adobe structure had three storeys. On the first were workrooms in which Indians plied their crafts and goods for sale were displayed. The second storey contained the Fred Harvey Collection of Navajo Weaving, an exhibition of baskets and other artefacts. On the top floor were rooms for the accommodation of the Hopi who lived and worked on site. The whole was designed by Mary Colter, who was to become the company's architect and interior designer, working almost invariably from Indian motifs.[14]

As well as appearing in villages recreated on Harvey premises, Pueblo Indians also became living exhibits at the international expositions that were so popular at the time. For example, the ATSF sponsored 'The Painted Desert', a ten-acre site at the 1915 Panama-California Exposition in San Diego. Specially constructed on the site were buildings in the style of the pueblos at Zuni and Taos, and an assembly of nearly 300 Indians from the south-west, making pottery, baskets and silverware.[15]

In 1926 the Harvey Company began its Indian Detours. Tourists disembarked from ATSF trains at stations in Albuquerque or Santa Fe and were transported by car on a trip round the area, taking in various Indian pueblos on the way. The Detours offered a privileged experience, guided by young white women themselves costumed in Indian style:

When you detrain anywhere for a Harveycar Indian-detour, one of us will greet you on the platform. There won't be any difficulty in recognizing our uniform, with its brilliant Navajo blouse, flashing Navajo belt of figured silver conchos, turquoise and squash-blossom necklaces, and the Thunderbird emblem on a soft outing hat. From that moment we want you to feel at home in the South-west – not as a tourist to be bundled about, but as part of a little group on a private exploration where one of the party knows and loves the country and is going to do her utmost to make you revel in every hour you spend in it.[16]

The Detours were publicized through lectures accompanied by lantern slides. Inevitably, what was presented was a heavily skewed view of the Indians:

In a swirl of color, and completely removed from their original ethnographic context, the slides of the Indian Detours reinforced the cultural stereotypes of Pueblo peoples. They glossed over the differences among Pueblo groups and concentrated on aspects of their domestic life that highlighted the differences between middle-class European Americans and Pueblo families. Because the images were grounded in the ordered materiality of the economics of family production, tourists could easily see cultural differences. The slides reinforce a timeless vision of the Pueblo Indians centered on craft production in a civil but primitive environment. The overall effect is to suggest that, although Indians are different from them, tourists have nothing to fear from them. While producing goods for a European American economy, Pueblo people are gracious, smiling, trusting, civil, nonthreatening and family centered.[17]

One of the adjectives most frequently applied by white observers to Pueblo societies was 'timeless'. A Harvey Company brochure produced in 1928 writes: 'New Mexico's mystifying ruins were left by the oldest races in America. Her changeless inhabited Indian pueblos were rooted in antiquity before Columbus sailed.'[18] Because the Pueblo villages were old, older than the civilization of the whites who came to stand and stare, it seemed as if they had always been thus. Indian life was, it appeared, without history, either past or future. In fact, the people that the Indian Detours presented had undergone many changes as a result of their contact with whites. One effect of the Harvey Company's use of Indians to promote itself was that Indian production of artefacts was increasingly tailored to the market. Objects that had once had ritual or religious significance became commercial commodities, with the quantity and style of production depending on sales. Herman Schweizer, the manager of Fred Harvey's Indian Department, was in frequent contact with suppliers attempting to influence what was made. Thus he wrote to J. L. Hubbell, manager of a trading post:

By the way, can't you arrange to use more of the brown wool in your blankets? People are getting tired of the

'Pueblo Indian drilling turquoise, New Mexico', a Fred Harvey postcard.

grey body blankets with black & white designs. We have got to get up something new all the time to keep the public interested so they will buy. This is good business for you as well as us.[19]

Schweizer also influenced the style of jewellery (silver jewellery was in fact an art that the Indians adopted only after the arrival of the Spanish): 'Native American silversmiths were encouraged to make jewelry forms such as brooches, earrings, and pendants that were not typically made and worn by south-western Native Americans but were compatible in form to jewelry worn by Euro-Americans during the early 1900s.'[20]

One can for the most part only guess at the responses of the Indians themselves to being exhibits in a show arranged for the entertainment of visitors to the south-west, but some comments have survived. Rina Swentzell from Santa Clara Pueblo recounted in 1995:

> I got this real sense . . . even as a child watching the buses coming in, the feeling of – we were not good enough, ourselves as people were not good enough, everything about us was not good enough . . . It was taking away our sense of self. It was not giving us any sense of pride because we were making pottery. It didn't leave us with something special and something really incredibly beautiful but it was exposure to that other world, exposure to money, exposure to that other world made us feel less than adequate. We were made to feel totally devalued. As money was becoming valued, our culture, ourselves, our way of life was devalued.[21]

The commodification of Indian production, the introduction of money and the bringing of the Indians into the white economy, albeit with a marginal status, threatened to accomplish indirectly what government policy had often attempted by more direct means, the absorption of Indian societies into the mainstream and the loss of Indian identity. Sylvia Rodríguez has described a dual response to the experience of being on the receiving end of the tourist experience:

> On the one hand the native is seduced by his own glamorous image in the admiring eyes of the friendly new colonizers. He gains crucial insight into the Other's exploitable yearning. On the other hand, the new economy of authenticity offers fresh opportunity – perilous in its combination of allure and illusion . . . the native is caught in a constant tension between being controlled (taken in or trapped) by his romanticized image, on the one hand, and having control over and being able to use

Tourists at Zuni Pueblo, New Mexico, c. 1890.

it effectively, on the other. Successful manipulation of the image without succumbing to it is a tricky and dangerous business that requires a delicate mix of scepticism, separatism, and at least qualified good faith. This creates a split, I propose, between the self offered up to or hunted down by the tourist gaze and the self who tries to live where the gaze cannot penetrate.

The situation in Taos thus has encouraged a kind of dual or double ethnicity . . . by which natives have come to enact and recognize a distinction between cultural practice for themselves and cultural practice exposed to the all-consuming tourist gaze.[22]

This articulates precisely the sense I had in the encounter with a Taos Indian that I described at the beginning of this book: that the Indian existed in two worlds, one of which I might also inhabit, the other which would remain impenetrable to me. We have to recognize that for white people our view of Indians is always going to be one coloured by the assumptions we bring with us. Yet for the first half of the twentieth century an alternative view of Indians became established in white culture, one which was still a representation of Indians by others, rather than a self-representation, but which nevertheless presented a different model from the screaming savage of popular literature and film.

Hollywood, however, was not interested. Rendering the south-west safe for tourism, processing its wildness into a 'land of enchantment', produced a marketable commodity, but one that held little appeal for Hollywood, which required instead that its Indians constitute a threat, albeit one safely neutralized in the present. Only occasionally can Pueblo Indians be glimpsed in the cinema, providing a little local colour to a spectacle such as *The Harvey Girls* (1945), MGM's celebration of the profitable relationship between Fred Harvey and the ATSF. Significantly, the film is not a western but a musical, primarily interested in heterosexual romance, not in the conflict between wilderness and civilization, which it reduces to a contest between the raucous dance-hall girls on one side of the street and the demure Harvey waitresses handing out coffee and steaks on the other. The film's best-known song, belted out by Harvey girl Judy Garland, is 'On the Atchison, Topeka and the Santa Fe', a paean to the romantic allure and seducing comforts of the company's trains ('What a lovely trip, I'm feeling so fresh and alive/And I'm so glad to arrive,' trills Judy as she alights). During the number, several Pueblo Indians can be seen, in the background or at the margins of the frame, colourfully dressed in bright shirts, headbands and silver-conch belts. The Indians are comfortably outnumbered by the cowboys on hand to greet Judy, and reassuringly the Indians are a family group, with both women and children present. Far from being a threat, as the conflict-orientated formula of the Western requires, Indians here are simply a part of the tourist experience. As Remington remarked, they were 'too tame', and now that the railroad had arrived, within reach of any 'tenderfoot'.

references

introduction

1 Philip J. Deloria, 'Historiography', *A Companion to American Indian History*, ed. Philip J. Deloria and Neal Salisbury (Oxford, 2004), p. 6.

2 Edward Said, *Orientalism* (London, 1978).

3 Paul B. Armstrong, quoted in Mick Gidley, ed., *Representing Others: White Views of Indigenous Peoples* (Exeter, 1992), pp. 8–9.

4 Alexandra Harmon, 'Wanted: More Histories of Indian Identity', in Deloria and Salisbury, *Companion to American Indian History*, p. 255.

5 Lee Irwin, 'Native American Spirituality: History, Theory, and Reformulation', in Deloria and Salisbury, *Companion to American Indian History*, p. 114.

6 Shari M. Huhndorf, *Going Native: Indians in the American Cultural Imagination* (Ithaca, NY, 2001), p. 161.

7 National Museum of the American Indian, *Map and Guide* (London, 2004), p. 7.

8 Duane Blue Spruce, ed., *Spirit of a Native Place* (Washington, DC, 2004), p. 56.

9 *Map and Guide*, p. 50.

10 Ibid., p. 39.

11 *New York Times*, 21 September 2004.

12 Taken from the author's notes.

13 Ralph E. Friar and Natasha Friar, *The Only Good Indian . . . the Hollywood Gospel* (New York, 1972).

14 John A. Price, in Gretchen M. Bataille and Charles L. P. Silet, eds,

The Pretend Indians: Images of Native Americans in the Movies (Ames, IA, 1980), p. 87.

15 Ward Churchill, *Fantasies of the Master Race: Literature, Cinema and the Colonization of American Indians* (Monroe, ME, 1992).

16 Quoted in Armando José Prats, *Invisible Natives: Myth & Identity in the American Western* (Ithaca, NY, 2002), p. 251.

17 Jacquelyn Kilpatrick, *Celluloid Indians: Native Americans and Film* (Lincoln, NE, 1999); Peter C. Rollins and John E. O'Connor, eds, *Hollywood's Indian: The Portrayal of the Native American in Film* (Lexington, KY, 1998).

1 the formation of a genre

1 See Edward Buscombe, ed., *The BFI Companion to the Western* (London, 1988).

2 Colin G. Calloway, *One Vast Winter Count: The Native American West before Lewis and Clark* (Lincoln, NE, 2003), p. 98.

3 Ibid., p. 275.

4 Ibid., p. 284.

5 Montrose J. Moses, ed., *Representative Plays by American Dramatists* (New York, 1918), pp. 594–5.

6 Terrence Malick's beautiful and subtle *The New World* (2006) is the latest, but almost certainly not the last, version of this mythic story.

7 Rosemary K. Bank, *Theatre Culture in America 1825–1860* (Cambridge, 1997), p. 66.

8 Richard Moody, ed., *Metamora*, reprinted in *Dramas from the American Theatre 1762–1907* (Bloomington, IN, 1966), p. 210.

9 Ibid., p. 226.

10 George Catlin, *Letters and Notes on the Manners, Customs, and Conditions of the North American Indians*, 1 (London, 1844; repr. New York, 1973), p. 16.

11 Kathryn Zabelle Derounian-Stodola, ed., *Women's Indian Captivity Narratives* (Harmondsworth, 1998), p. xv.

12 Linda Colley, *Captives: Britain, Empire and the World, 1600–1850* (London, 2003), p. 147.

13 James Fenimore Cooper, *The Last of the Mohicans* (1826; repr. New York, 1962), p. 122.

14 Howard R. Lamar, ed., *The New Encyclopedia of the American West* (New Haven, CT, 1998), p. 545.

15 Bill Brown, ed., *Reading the West: An Anthology of Dime Westerns* (Boston, MA, and New York, 1997), p. 175.

16 Ibid., p. 202.

17 Ibid., pp. 278–9.

18 Ibid., p. 298.

19 Ibid., p. 27.

20 See Alex Nemerov, '"Doing the 'Old America'": The Image of the American West 1880–1920', in *The West as America: Reinterpreting Images of the Frontier, 1820–1920*, ed. William H. Truettner (Washington, DC, 1991), pp. 307–9.

21 Don Russell, *The Lives and Legends of Buffalo Bill* (Norman, OK, 1960), pp. 376–7.

22 L. G. Moses, *Wild West Shows and the Images of American Indians, 1883–1933* (Albuquerque, NM, 1996), p. 77.

23 For this episode in Cody's life, see Paul L. Hedren, 'The Contradictory Legacies of Buffalo Bill Cody's First Scalp for Custer', *Montana: The Magazine of Western History*, LV/1 (Spring 2005), pp. 16–17.

24 Quoted in Henry Nash Smith, *Virgin Land: The American West as Symbol and Myth* (New York, 1950), p. 119.

25 Moses, *Wild West Shows*, p. 44.

26 See Christopher M. Lyman, *The Vanishing Race and Other Illusions: Photographs of Indians by Edward S. Curtis* (New York, 1982), pp. 70–71.

27   Quoted in ibid., p. 79.

28   Brian W. Dippie, *The Vanishing American: White Attitudes and US Indian Policy* (Lawrence, KS, 1982).

29   Ibid., p. 1.

30   Ibid., p. 15.

31   Henry Wadsworth Longfellow, *The Song of Hiawatha* (1855), canto XXI, 'The White Man's Foot', lines 110–31.

32   Quoted in Dippie, *The Vanishing American*, p. 213.

33   See Renato Rosaldo, *Culture and Truth: The Remaking of Social Analysis* (Boston, MA, 1993).

34   Jon Tuska and Vicki Piekarski, eds, *Encyclopedia of Frontier and Western Fiction* (New York, 1983), p. 129.

35   Zane Grey, *The Vanishing American* (New York, 1991), p. 329.

36   Moses, *Wild West Shows*, p. 74.

37   Quoted in Angela Aleiss, *Making the White Man's Indian: Native Americans and Hollywood Movies* (Westport, CT, 2005), p. 5.

38   See Scott Simmon, *The Invention of the Western Film: A Cultural History of the Genre's First Half-Century* (Cambridge, 2003), p. 17.

39   Advertisement quoted in Aleiss, *Making the White Man's Indian*, p. 7.

40   Richard Abel, '"Our Country"/Whose Country? The "Americanisation" Project of Early Westerns', in *Back in the Saddle Again: New Essays on the Western*, ed. Edward Buscombe and Roberta E. Pearson (London, 1998), p. 84.

41   See Andrew Brodie Smith, *Shooting Cowboys and Indians: Silent Western Films, American Culture, and the Birth of Hollywood* (Boulder, CO, 2003), pp. 79–80.

42   Simmon, *The Invention of the Western Film*, p. 31.

43   See Smith, *Shooting Cowboys and Indians*, p. 97.

44   Simmon, *The Invention of the Western Film*, pp. 36–7.

45   See Joseph McBride, *Searching for John Ford: A Life* (London, 2003), p. 505.

2 the liberal western

1   Brian W. Dippie, *The Vanishing American: White Attitudes and US Indian Policy* (Lawrence, KS, 1982), p. 15.

2   See Robert F. Berkhofer, Jr, *The White Man's Indian: Images of the American Indian from Columbus to the Present* (New York, 1979), p. 54.

3   Quoted in Dippie, *The Vanishing American*, p. 109.

4   R. David Edmunds, 'Native Americans and the United States, Canada and Mexico', in *A Companion to American Indian History*, ed. Philip J. Deloria and Neal Salisbury (Oxford, 2004), p. 401.

5   Steve Neale, 'Vanishing Americans: Racial and Ethnic Issues in the Interpretation and Context of Post-war "Pro-Indian" Westerns', in *Back in the Saddle Again: New Essays on the Western*, ed. Edward Buscombe and Roberta E. Pearson (London, 1998).

6   See ibid., n. 61, p. 27.

7   Jay Silverheels played the role twice more, in *The Battle at Apache Pass* (1952) and *Walk the Proud Land* (1956), besides achieving substantial fame playing Tonto in the television series *The Lone Ranger*.

8   Scott Simmon, *The Invention of the Western Film: A Cultural History of the Genre's First Half-Century* (Cambridge, 2003), p. 70.

9   Eleanor Leacock, quoted in Berkhofer, *The White Man's Indian*, p. 67.

10 Angela Aleiss, *Making the White Man's Indian: Native Americans and Hollywood Movies* (Westport, CT, 2005), p. 133.

11 Shari M. Huhndorf, *Going Native: Indians in the American Cultural Imagination* (Ithaca, NY, 2001), p. 4.

12 Ibid., p. 5.

13 Thomas King, *Green Grass, Running Water* (New York, 1994), p. 216.

14 Costner's activities in South Dakota are discussed on several websites, including http://www.ratical.org/ratville/KC.html.

15 See Laura Mulvey, Dirk Snauwaert and Mark Alice Durant, eds,

Jimmie Durham (London, n. d.), p. 38.

16 See http://www.hulleah.com/ and see also Lucy R. Lippard, ed., *Partial Recall: Photographs of Native North Americans* (New York, 1992).

17 Beverly R. Singer, *Wiping the War Paint off the Lens: Native American Film and Video* (Minneapolis, MN, 2001).

18 Sherman Alexie, *The Lone Ranger and Tonto Fistfight in Heaven* (New York, 1993).

3 passing as an indian

1   Iron Eyes Cody [as told to Collin Perry], *Iron Eyes: My Life as a Hollywood Indian* (London, 1982), p. 30.

2   www.adcouncil.org/campaigns/historic_campaigns_pollution/

3   Cody, *Iron Eyes*, p. 16.

4   New Orleans *Times-Picayune*, 26 May 1996.

5   Edward Buscombe, ed., *The BFI Companion to the Western* (London, 1988), p. 332.

6   Both are quoted in www.newtimesla.com/1999/040899/feature1-4.html

7   Cody, *Iron Eyes*, p. 195.

8   Season 4, episode 42, first transmitted on HBO, 29 September 2002.

9   Thomas King, *Green Grass, Running Water* (New York, 1994), pp. 166–7.

10 Louis Owens, *Dark River* (Norman, OK, 1999), pp. 96–7.

11 Richard Willis, *Movie Pictorial*, 13 June 1914.

12 http://www.homesteadmuseum.org/

13 Nancy Cook, 'The Scandal of Race: Authenticity, *The Silent Enemy* and the Problem of Long Lance', in *Headline Hollywood: A Century of Film Scandal*, ed. Adrienne L. McLean and David A. Cook (New Brunswick, NJ, 2001).

14 See Philip J. Deloria, *Playing Indian* (New Haven, CT, 1998), *passim*.

15 Shari M. Huhndorf, *Going Native: Indians in the American Cultural Imagination* (Ithaca, NY, 2001), p. 71.

16 Deloria, *Playing Indian*, p. 113.

17 Ibid., p. 131.

18 See Hugh Honour, *The New Golden Land: European Images from the Discoveries to the Present Time* (London, 1976), pp. 245–7.

19 Linda Colley, *Captives: Britain, Empire and the World, 1600–1850* (London, 2003), pp. 188–9.

20 http://www.nypl.org/research/chss/spe/rbk/faids/highwatr.html.

21 There are several internet sources for this affair; for example, http://www.newsoftheodd.com/article1027.html.

22 For an authoritative summary of the case of Chief Seattle, see the National Archives web entry at http://www.archives.gov/publications/prologue/1985/spring/chief-seattle.html.

23 See Colin G. Calloway, *One Vast Winter Count: The Native American West before Lewis and Clark* (Lincoln, NE, 2003), p. 220: 'the Hurons had exterminated their own beavers by 1635'.

24 For example, Jared Diamond argues that the Maya Indians of Central America destroyed their highly advanced civilization, leading to catastrophe by the tenth century AD as a result of deforestation and consequent soil erosion. See Jared Diamond, *Collapse: How Societies Choose to Fail or Succeed* (New York, 2005).

25 Huhndorf, *Going Native*, pp. 129–30.

4 indians in the european western

1 See Hugh Honour, *The New Golden Land: European Images from the Discoveries to the Present Time* (London, 1976), p. 5.

2 Ibid., p. 12.

3 Ibid., p. 6.

4   Ray Allen Billington, *Land of Savagery, Land of Promise: The European Image of the American Frontier* (New York, 1981), p. 24.

5   Ibid., pp. 110–11.

6   Ibid., p. 111.

7   Ibid., p. 112.

8   Ibid., p. 113.

9   Ibid., p. 123.

10 For some sales figures, see Tassilo Schneider, 'Finding a New *Heimat* in the Wild West: Karl May and the German Western of the 1960s', in *Back in the Saddle Again: New Essays on the Western*, ed. Edward Buscombe and Roberta E. Pearson (London, 1998), p. 143.

11 http://www.kirjasto.sci.fi/karlmay.htm.

12 Gerd Gemünden, 'Between Karl May and Karl Marx: The DEFA *Indianerfilme*', in *Germans and Indians: Fantasies, Encounters, Projections*, ed. Colin G. Calloway, Gerd Gemünden and Suzanne Zantop (Lincoln, NE, 2002), p. 247.

13 *Germans and Indians*, p. 37.

14 Ibid., p. 187.

15 Ibid., p. 190.

16 Karl May, *Winnetou*, trans. and abridged David Koblick (Pullman, WA, 1999), p. 62.

17 Ibid., p. 138.

18 Ibid., p. 140.

19 Ibid., p. 115.

20 Ibid., p. 1.

21 See http://www.karl-may-stiftung.de/ and links.

22 Schneider, 'Finding a New *Heimat* in the Wild West', p. 149.

23 Quoted in Brian W. Dippie, *Catlin and his Contemporaries: The Politics of Patronage* (Lincoln, NE, 1990), p. 56.

24 Billington, *Land of Savagery, Land of Promise*, p. 140.

25 Ibid., p. 141.

26 Ibid., p. 141.

27 Ibid., p. 147.

28 Ibid., p. 146.

29 Quoted in Edward Buscombe, 'Photographing the Indian', in *Back in the Saddle Again*, p. 33.

30 Dippie, *Catlin and his Contemporaries*, p. 99.

31 Paul Reddin, *Wild West Shows* (Urbana and Chicago, IL, 1999), p. 32.

32 Ibid., p. 33.

33 Dippie, *Catlin and his Contemporaries*, p. 101.

34 Reddin, *Wild West Shows*, p. 41.

35 Quoted in Edward Buscombe and Kevin Mulroy, 'The Western Worldwide', in *Western Amerykanski: Polish Poster Art and the Western*, ed. Kevin Mulroy (Seattle, WA, 1999), p. 4.

36 Dippie, *Catlin and his Contemporaries*, pp. 119–20.

37 Quoted in Buscombe and Mulroy, 'The Western Worldwide', p. 6.

38 Billington, *Land of Savagery, Land of Promise*, p. 50.

39 Quoted in Buscombe and Mulroy, 'The Western Worldwide', p. 21.

40 Luke McKernan, unpublished paper.

41 Christopher Frayling, *Sergio Leone: Something to Do with Death* (London, 2000), p. 141.

42 Schneider, 'Finding a New *Heimat* in the Wild West', p. 142.

43 Christopher Frayling, *Spaghetti Westerns: Cowboys and Europeans from Karl May to Sergio Leone* (London, 1981), p. 103.

44 Gemünden, 'Between Karl May and Karl Marx', pp. 250–51.

45 Katrin Sieg, 'Indian Impersonation as Historical Surrogation', in *Germans and Indians: Fantasies, Encounters, Projections*, ed. Colin G. Calloway, Gerd Gemünden and Suzanne Zantop (Lincoln, NE, 2002), p. 220.

46 Gemünden, 'Between Karl May and Karl Marx', p. 249.

47 Sieg, 'Indian Impersonation as Historical Surrogation', p. 230.

48 See http://en.wikipedia.org/wiki/Blueberry_(comic).

49 http://www.disneylandparis.com/uk/disney_village/having_fun/
sound_indian.htm.

5 indians not injuns

1 Quoted in William H. Truettner, 'Science and Sentiment: Indian
Images at the Turn of the Century', in *Art in New Mexico, 1900-
1945: Paths to Taos and Santa Fe*, exh. cat., ed. Charles C. Eldredge,
Julie Schimmel and William H. Truettner, National Museum of
American Art (Washington, DC, 1986), p. 22.

2 Ibid., p. 24.

3 Sherry Clayton Tagget and Ted Schwarz, *Paintbrushes and Pistols:
How the Taos Artists Sold the West* (Santa Fe, NM, 1990), p. 67.

4 Sandra D'Emilio and Suzan Campbell, *Visions and Visionaries:
The Art and Artists of the Santa Fe Railway* (Salt Lake City, UT,
1991), p. 86.

5 Richard Frost, quoted in Barbara A. Babcock, 'First Families:
Gender, Reproduction, and the Mythic Southwest', in Marta Weigle
and Barbara A. Babcock, *The Great Southwest of the Fred Harvey
Company and the Santa Fe Railway* (Phoenix, AZ, 1996), p. 217.

6 Quoted in William H. Truettner, 'The Art of Pueblo Life', in *Art in
New Mexico*, p. 67.

7 Quoted in D'Emilio and Campbell, *Visions and Visionaries*, p. 111.

8 Peggy Samuels and Harold Samuels, *Frederic Remington: A
Biography* (Garden City, NY, 1982), p. 307.

9 Ibid., p. 307.

10 T. C. McLuhan, *Dream Tracks: The Railroad and the American
Indian, 1890–1930* (New York, 1985), p. 31.

11 Quoted in Truettner, *Art in New Mexico*, p. 28.

12 Peter B. Hales, *William Henry Jackson and the Transformation of the
American Landscape* (Philadelphia, 1988), p. 266.

13 Postcard in the author's possession.

14 See Matilda McQuaid with Karen Bartlett, 'Building an Image of the Southwest: Mary Colter, Fred Harvey Company Architect', in Weigle and Babcock, *The Great Southwest*, p. 26.

15 Phoebe S. Kropp, '"There Is a Little Sermon in That": Constructing the Native Southwest at the San Diego Panama-California Exposition of 1915', in Weigle and Babcock, *The Great Southwest*, p. 36.

16 Marta Weigle, '"Insisted on Authenticity": Harveycar Indian Detours, 1925–1931', in Weigle and Babcock, *The Great Southwest*, p. 58.

17 Ibid., p. 52.

18 Truettner, in *Art in New Mexico*, p. 81.

19 Kathleen L. Howard and Diana F. Pardue, *Inventing the Southwest: The Fred Harvey Company and Native American Art* (Flagstaff, AZ, 1996), p. 45.

20 Ibid., p. 48.

21 Ibid., pp. 126–8.

22 Sylvia Rodríguez, 'The Tourist Gaze, Gentrification, and the Commodification of Subjectivity in Taos', in *Essays on the Changing Images of the Southwest*, ed. Richard Francaviglia and David Narrett (College Station, TX, 1994), p. 117.

select bibliography

Aleiss, Angela, *Making the White Man's Indian: Native Americans and Hollywood Movies* (Westport, CT, 2005)

Bataille, Gretchen M., and Charles L. P. Silet, eds, *The Pretend Indians: Images of Native Americans in the Movies* (Ames, IA, 1980)

Berkhofer Jr, Robert F., *The White Man's Indian: Images of the American Indian from Columbus to the Present* (New York, 1979)

Billington, Ray Allen, *Land of Savagery, Land of Promise: The European Image of the American Frontier* (New York, 1981)

Bird, S. Elizabeth, ed., *Dressing in Feathers: The Construction of the Indian in American Popular Culture* (Boulder, CO, 1996)

Bordewich, Fergus M., *Killing the White Man's Indian: Reinventing Native Americans at the End of the Twentieth Century* (New York, 1996)

Brown, Bill, ed., *Reading the West: An Anthology of Dime Westerns* (Boston, MA, and New York, 1997)

Buscombe, Edward, ed., *The BFI Companion to the Western* (London, 1988)

—, and Roberta E. Pearson, eds, *Back in the Saddle Again: New Essays on the Western* (London, 1998)

Calloway, Colin G., *One Vast Winter Count: The Native American West before Lewis and Clark* (Lincoln, NE, 2003)

—, Gerd Gemünden and Suzanne Zantop, eds, *Germans and Indians: Fantasies, Encounters, Projections* (Lincoln, NE, 2002)

Catlin, George, *Letters and Notes on the Manners, Customs, and Conditions of the North American Indians* (London, 1844, repr. New York, 1973)

Churchill, Ward, *Fantasies of the Master Race: Literature, Cinema and the Colonization of American Indians* (Monroe, ME, 1992)

Cody, Iron Eyes, *Iron Eyes: My Life as a Hollywood Indian* (London, 1982)

Colley, Linda, *Captives: Britain, Empire and the World, 1600–1850* (London, 2003)

Deloria, Philip J., *Playing Indian* (New Haven, CT, 1998)

—, and Neal Salisbury, eds, *A Companion to American Indian History* (Oxford, 2004)

D'Emilio, Sandra, and Suzan Campbell, *Visions and Visionaries: The Art and Artists of the Santa Fe Railway* (Salt Lake City, UT, 1991)

Derounian-Stodola, Kathryn Zabelle, ed., *Women's Indian Captivity Narratives* (Harmondsworth, 1998)

Dippie, Brian W., *The Vanishing American: White Attitudes and US Indian Policy* (Lawrence, KS, 1982)

—, *Catlin and his Contemporaries: The Politics of Patronage* (Lincoln, NE, 1990)

Drinnon, Richard, *Facing West: The Metaphysics of Indian-Hating and Empire-Building* (New York, 1980)

Eldredge, Charles C., Julie Schimmel and William H. Truettner, eds, *Art in New Mexico, 1900–1945: Paths to Taos and Santa Fe*, exh. cat., National Museum of American Art (Washington, DC, 1986)

Fiedler, Leslie A., *The Return of the Vanishing American* (London, 1968)

Flannery, Tim, *The Eternal Frontier: An Ecological History of North America and its Peoples* (London, 2001)

Francaviglia, Richard, and David Narrett, eds, *Essays on the Changing Images of the Southwest* (College Station, TX, 1994)

Frayling, Christopher, *Spaghetti Westerns: Cowboys and Europeans from Karl May to Sergio Leone* (London, 1981)

—, *Sergio Leone: Something to Do with Death* (London, 2000)

Friar, Ralph E., and Natasha Friar, *The Only Good Indian . . . The Hollywood Gospel* (New York, 1972)

Gidley, Mick, ed., *Representing Others: White Views of Indigenous Peoples* (Exeter, 1992)

Hales, Peter B., *William Henry Jackson and the Transformation of the American Landscape* (Philadelphia, 1988)

Honour, Hugh, *The New Golden Land: European Images from the Discoveries to the Present Time* (London, 1976)

Howard, Kathleen L., and Diana F. Pardue, *Inventing the Southwest: The Fred Harvey Company and Native American Art* (Flagstaff, AZ, 1996)

Huhndorf, Shari M., *Going Native: Indians in the American Cultural Imagination* (Ithaca, NY, 2001)

Jennings, Francis, *The Invasion of America: Indians, Colonialism and the Cant of Conquest* (New York, 1976)

Kilpatrick, Jacquelyn, *Celluloid Indians: Native Americans and Film* (Lincoln, NE, 1999)

Lippard, Lucy R., ed., *Partial Recall: Photographs of Native North Americans* (New York, 1992)

Lyman, Christopher M., *The Vanishing Race and Other Illusions: Photographs of Indians by Edward S. Curtis* (New York, 1982)

McLuhan, T. C., *Dream Tracks: The Railroad and the American Indian, 1890–1930* (New York, 1985)

Matthiessen, Peter, *Indian Country* (London, 1986)

May, Karl, *Winnetou*, trans. and abridged David Koblick (Pullman, WA, 1999)

Moses, L. G., *Wild West Shows and the Images of American Indians, 1883–1933* (Albuquerque, NM, 1996)

Kevin Mulroy, ed., *Western Amerykanski: Polish Poster Art and the Western* (Seattle, WA, 1999)

Prats, Armando José, *Invisible Natives: Myth & Identity in the American Western* (Ithaca, NY, 2002)

Reddin, Paul, *Wild West Shows* (Urbana, IL, and Chicago, 1999)

Rollins, Peter C., and John E. O'Connor, eds, *Hollywood's Indian: The Portrayal of the Native American in Film* (Lexington, KY, 1998)

Russell, Don, *The Lives and Legends of Buffalo Bill* (Norman, OK, 1960)

Said, Edward, *Orientalism* (London, 1978)

Samuels, Peggy, and Harold Samuels, *Frederic Remington: A Biography* (Garden City, NY, 1982)

Shoemaker, Nancy, ed., *American Indians*, Blackwell Readers in American Social and Cultural History (Oxford, 2001)

Simmon, Scott, *The Invention of the Western Film: A Cultural History of the Genre's First Half-Century* (Cambridge, 2003)

Singer, Beverly R., *Wiping the War Paint off the Lens: Native American Film and Video* (Minneapolis, MN, 2001)

Smith, Andrew Brodie, *Shooting Cowboys and Indians: Silent Western Films, American Culture, and the Birth of Hollywood* (Boulder, CO, 2003)

Smith, Henry Nash, *Virgin Land: The American West as Symbol and Myth* (New York, 1950)

Tagget, Sherry Clayton, and Ted Schwarz, *Paintbrushes and Pistols: How the Taos Artists Sold the West* (Santa Fe, NM, 1990)

Todorov, Tzvetan. *The Conquest of America* (New York, 1984)

Truettner, William H., ed., *The West as America: Reinterpreting Images of the Frontier, 1820–1920* (Washington, DC, 1991)

Tuska, John, and Vicki Piekarski, eds, *Encyclopedia of Frontier and Western Fiction* (New York, 1983)

Weigle, Marta, and Barbara A. Babcock, eds, *The Great Southwest of the Fred Harvey Company and the Santa Fe Railway* (Phoenix, AZ, 1996)

acknowledgements

Thanks to Vivian Constantinopoulos for commissioning this book, for sticking with it and making some very helpful suggestions for improvement. Thanks also to Barry King, Peter Stanfield, Susan Kollin and Imogene Brunner for help of various kinds.

photo acknowledgements

The author and publishers wish to express their thanks to the below sources of illustrative material and/or permission to reproduce it. In some cases locations of works are given solely below, in the interests of brevity:

Brigham Young University Fine Arts Museum, Provo, Utah: p. 32; The Buffalo Bill Historical Center, Cody, Wyoming: pp. 58, 77 (foot), 225; Cincinnati Art Museum, Ohio: p. 56; Corcoran Gallery of Art, Massachusetts (gift of William Wilson Corcoran): p. 39; Eiteljorg Museum of American Indian and Western Art, Indianapolis, Indiana: p. 224; photos Library of Congress, Washington, DC (Prints and Photographs Division): pp. 68 (LC-USZ62-52411), 69 (Edward S. Curtis Collection, LC-DIG-ppmsca-05926); The Museum of Western Art, Denver, Colorado: p. 55; New York Public Library: p. 36; Phoenix Art Museum, Arizona: p. 57; Smithsonian Institution National Anthropological Archives, Suitland, Maryland (Bureau of American Ethnology Collection): p. 71 (photo Smithsonian Institution Photographic Services); The Sterling and Francine Clark Art Institute, Williamstown, Massachusetts: p. 54; University of Oklahoma Library, Norman, Oklahoma (Western History Collections, Frank Phillips Collection): p. 115; photo US National Archives, Washington, DC: p. 113; photo Adam Clark Vroman: p. 231; Wadsworth Atheneum, Hartford, Connecticut: pp. 35, 41; photo Ben Wittick: p. 241.

index

272